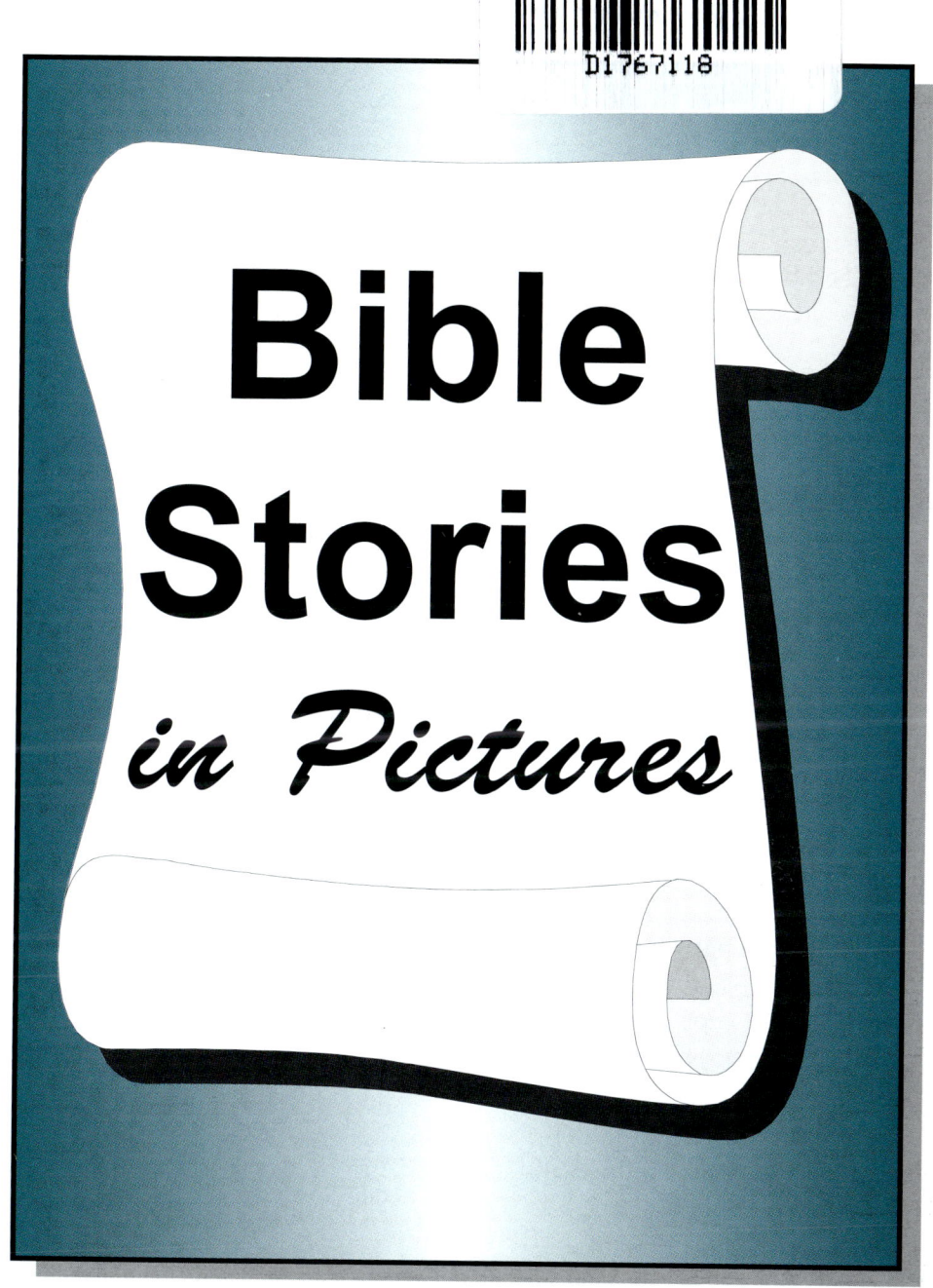

By William F. Beck

Published by: Multi-Language Publications Program
Board for World Missions
Wisconsin Evangelical Lutheran Synod
Milwaukee, Wisconsin

BIBLE STORIES IN PICTURES
Copyright ©2000 by WELS-BWM

Except for brief excerpts for review purposes, no part of this book may be reproduced or used in any form without written permission from the publisher.

Author: William F. Beck

Illustrators: Ruth W. Rogers
Marion J. Pabst
Judith McCormack

Cover and title pages and maps illustrator: Tyra Baumler
Main title page and table of contents illustrator: Michele Pfeifer

Revisions editor: Harold A. Essmann

First paperback printing, 2000
Second paperback printing, 2001

Printed in the United States
Winnebago Color Press, Menasha, Wisconsin

ISBN 0-9703210-0-7

Old Testament Stories

CREATION

In the Beginning
God Made Man
Adam and Eve Sin
Cain and Abel

NOAH

The Flood
Noah Leaves the Ark
The Rainbow

ABRAHAM

Abram Goes to Canaan
Lot Leaves Abram
Like the Stars
Sarah Laughs
The Angels Rescue Lot
King of the Philistines
Isaac and Ishmael
God Tests Abraham

MOSES

Birth of Moses
Moses Flees
The Burning Bush
Take Your Rod
Israel Leaves Egypt
In the Wilderness
Bread from Heaven
On Mount Sinai
Love God
Love Your Neighbor
The Golden Calf
Israel is Punished
Worship the Lord
The Copper Snake
Moses Dies

IN THE PROMISED LAND

Two Spies
Israel Crosses the Jordan
The Fall of Jericho
Joshua's Farewell
Deborah

RUTH

Naomi and Ruth
Boaz
Ruth Marries Boaz

THE KINGS

The Boy Samuel
Israel Wants a King
Samuel Anoints Saul
Samuel Anoints David
David and Goliath
King David
David Makes Solomon King

New Testament Stories

JESUS IS BORN

Gabriel Comes to Zacharias
Gabriel Comes to Mary
John is Born
Jesus is Born
The Angel Tells the Shepherds
The Wise Men
Jesus at Twelve

JESUS IS THE SON OF GOD

John Prepares the Way (Baptism)
Jesus Cleanses the Temple
The Samaritan Woman
At Home in Galilee
Preaching and Healing
Jesus Forgives Sin
The Son of God
Come to Me
Jesus Shows His Glory
The Light of the World

JESUS DIES AND LIVES

Gethsemane
Judas Betrays Jesus
Before Annas and Caiphas
Before Herod
See the Man
Jesus is Crucified
Jesus Dies
Jesus is Buried
Jesus Rises from the Dead
Jesus Lives
The Guards are Bribed
Behind Locked Doors
Breakfast with Jesus
Do You Love Me?
Jesus Goes up to Heaven

THE EARLY CHURCH

The Holy Spirit
Peter Tells about Jesus
The Lame Man
On Trial
Philip Baptizes a Treasurer

PAUL

Paul
Jesus Changes Paul
Antioch near Pisidia
A Message to Non-Jews
At Philippi
Thessalonica and Berea
Working Mightily
Paul the Missionary
Paul as Pastor
Paul's Last Days

Old Testament

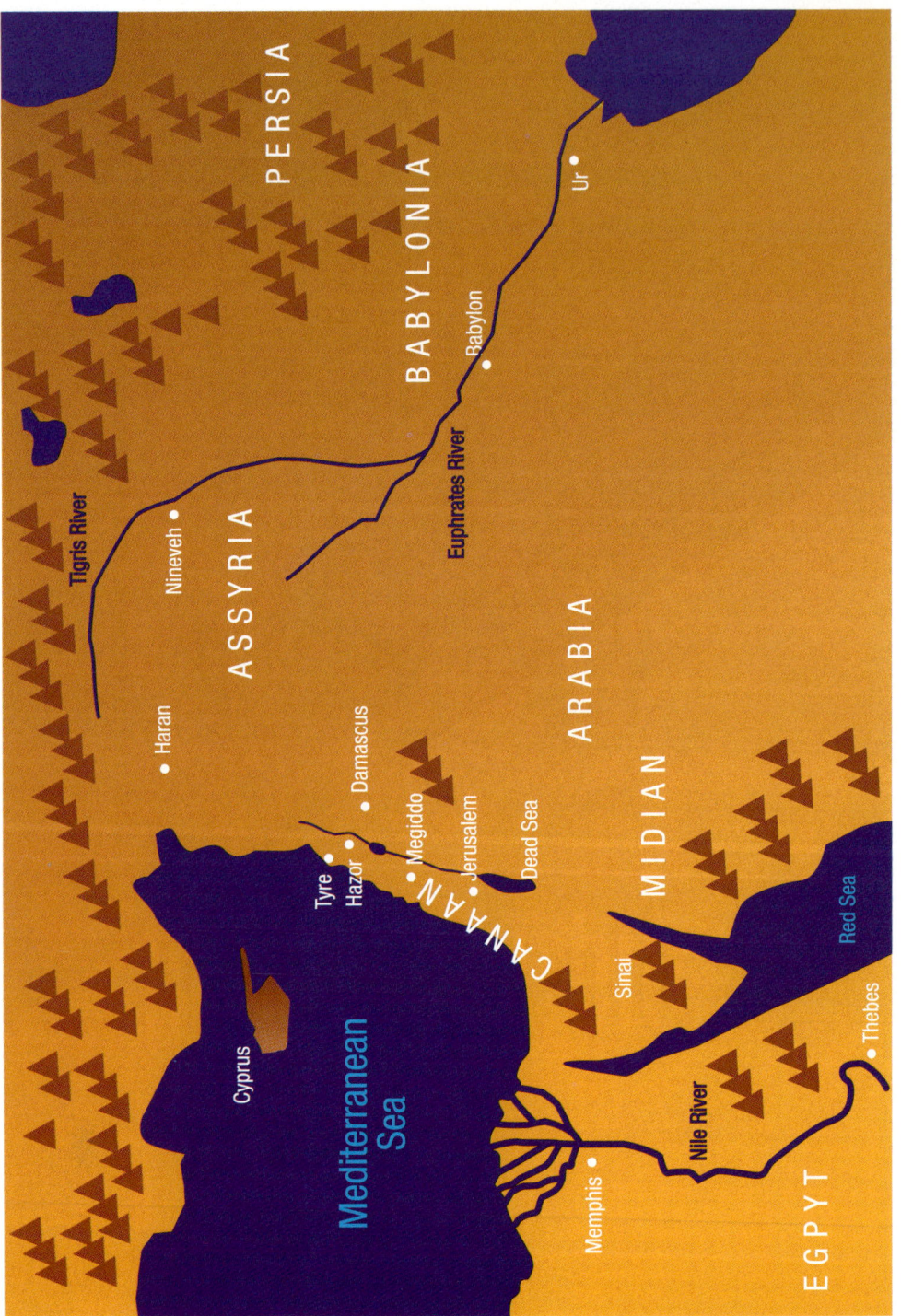

In the Beginning
GEN. 1:1-25; 2:4-6

BIBLE STORIES in PICTURES
by W. F. BECK
ILLUSTRATED BY RUTH W. ROGERS

GOD MADE THE HEAVENS AND THE EARTH

THE EARTH WAS WITHOUT FORM AND EMPTY

IT WAS DARK ON THE DEEP SEA. THE SPIRIT OF GOD MOVED OVER THE WATERS

THEN GOD SAID— **LET THERE BE LIGHT!** AND THERE WAS LIGHT.

GOD SAW THAT THE LIGHT WAS GOOD.

GOD SEPARATED THE LIGHT FROM THE DARKNESS. HE CALLED THE LIGHT DAY. HE CALLED THE DARKNESS NIGHT.

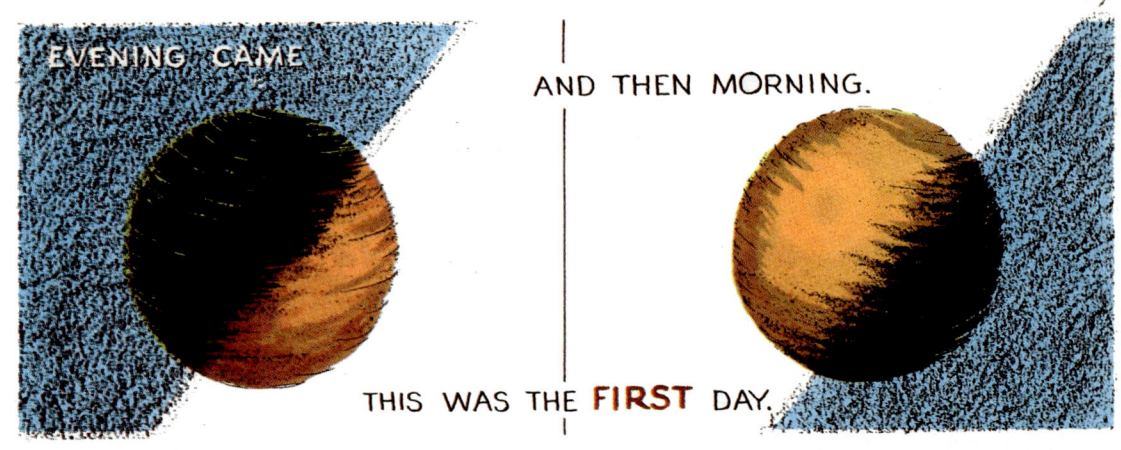

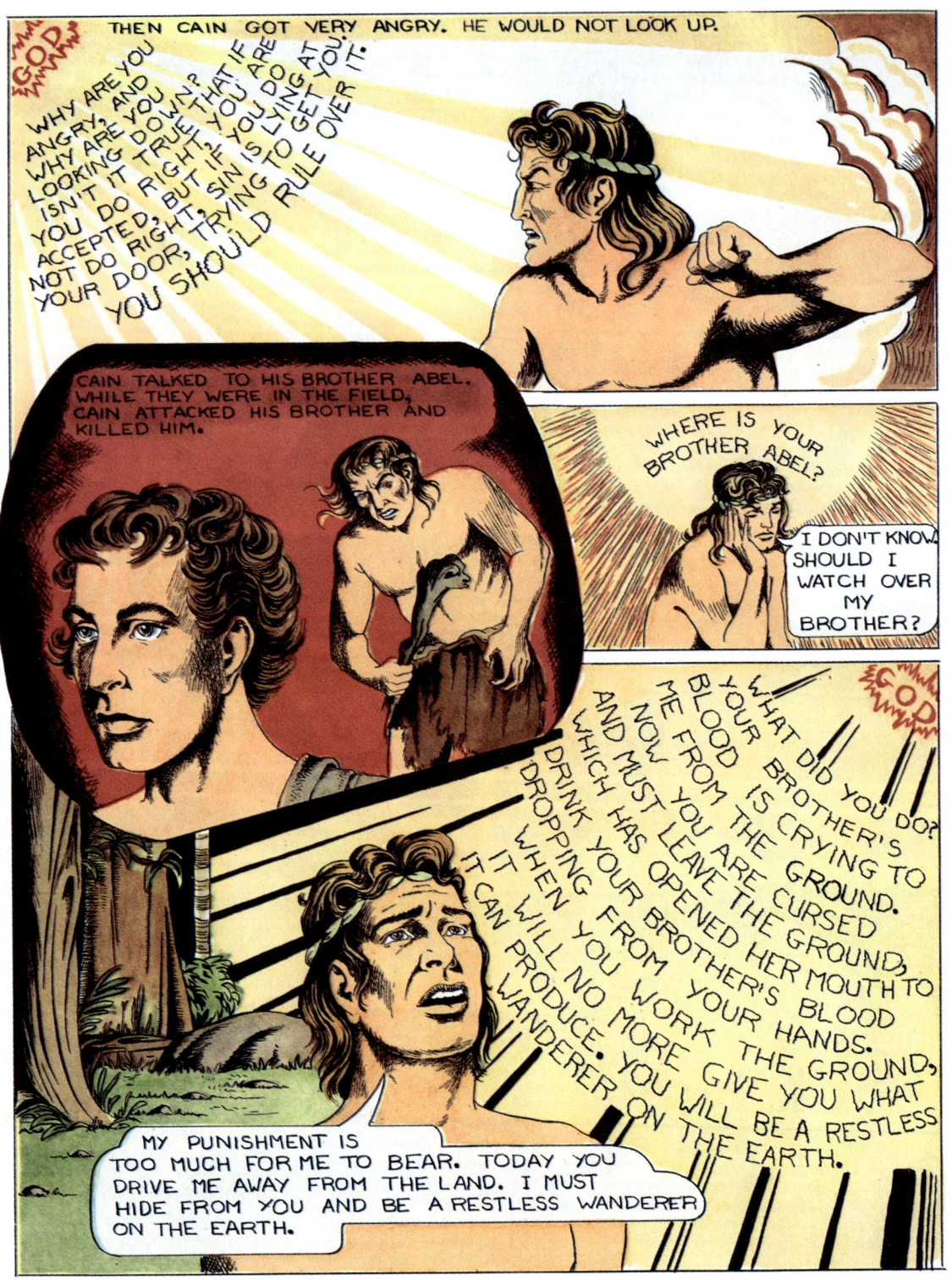

It rains for forty days. All life on earth is destroyed. Noah sees the water is disappearing. Finally, they can leave the ark.

A well known man of the Old Testament is Abraham. He is the father of many nations. He is also the ancestor of the Savior, Jesus.

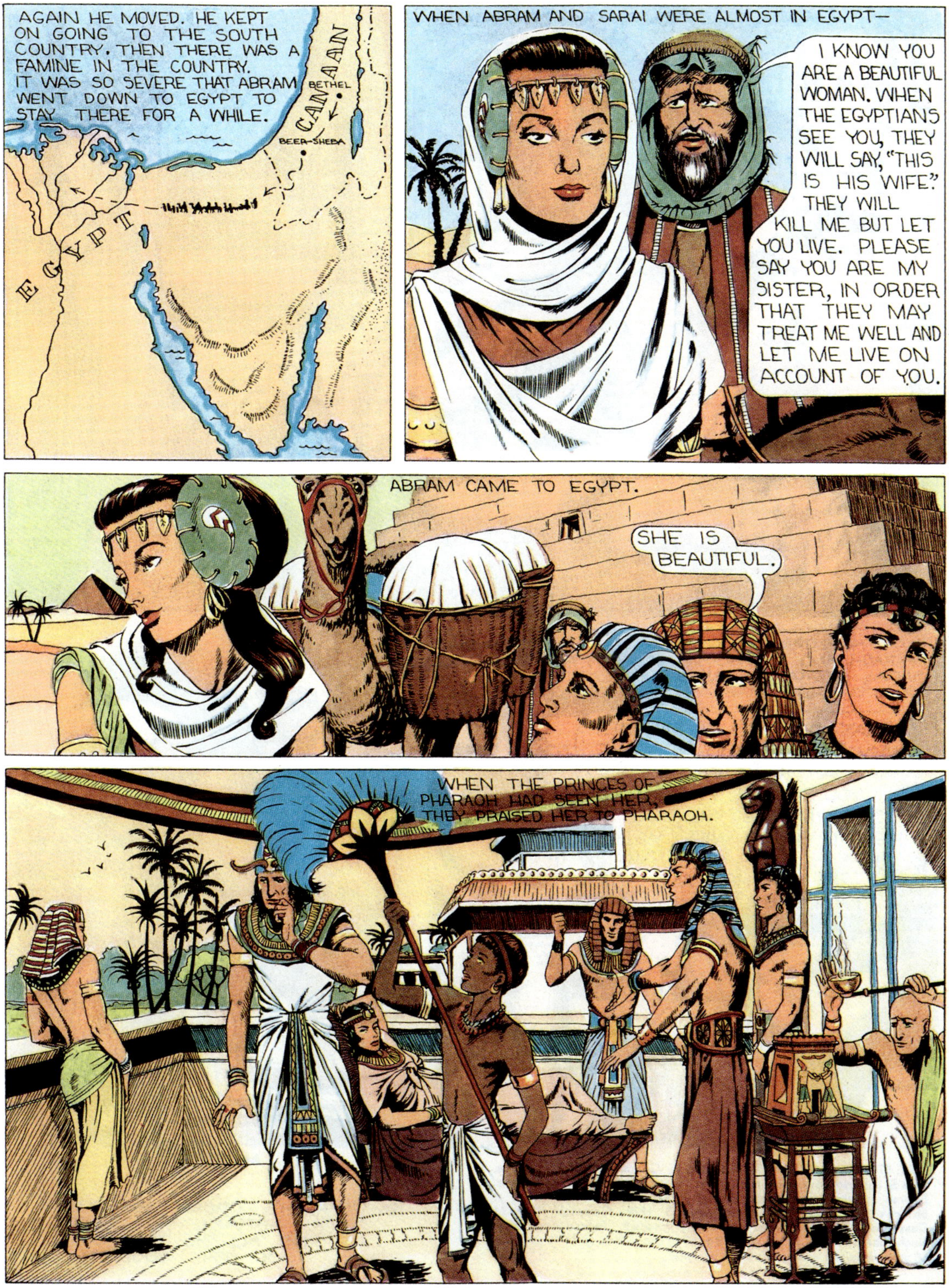

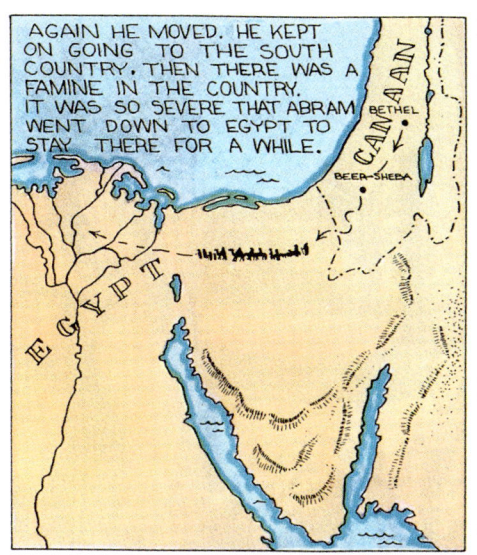

Abraham returns to Canaan. Fighting causes Abraham and Lot to live in different parts of the land. Abraham continues to worship the true God.

AFTER LOT HAD MOVED AWAY FROM ABRAM, THE LORD SPOKE TO ABRAM:

LOOK TO THE NORTH, SOUTH, EAST, AND WEST, BECAUSE ALL THE LAND YOU CAN SEE I WILL GIVE TO YOU AND TO YOUR DESCENDANTS FOREVER. GO AND TRAVEL THE LENGTH AND BREADTH OF THE LAND, BECAUSE I WILL GIVE IT TO YOU. I WILL GIVE YOU MANY DESCENDANTS LIKE THE DUST OF THE EARTH. IF ANYONE CAN COUNT THE DUST, YOUR DESCENDANTS ALSO CAN BE COUNTED.

ABRAM MOVED HIS TENTS. HE WENT TO LIVE AT HEBRON. THERE HE BUILT AN ALTAR TO THE LORD.

God promises to protect Abraham. God again promises Abraham will have many descendants. He promises Abraham his people will possess the land of Canaan.

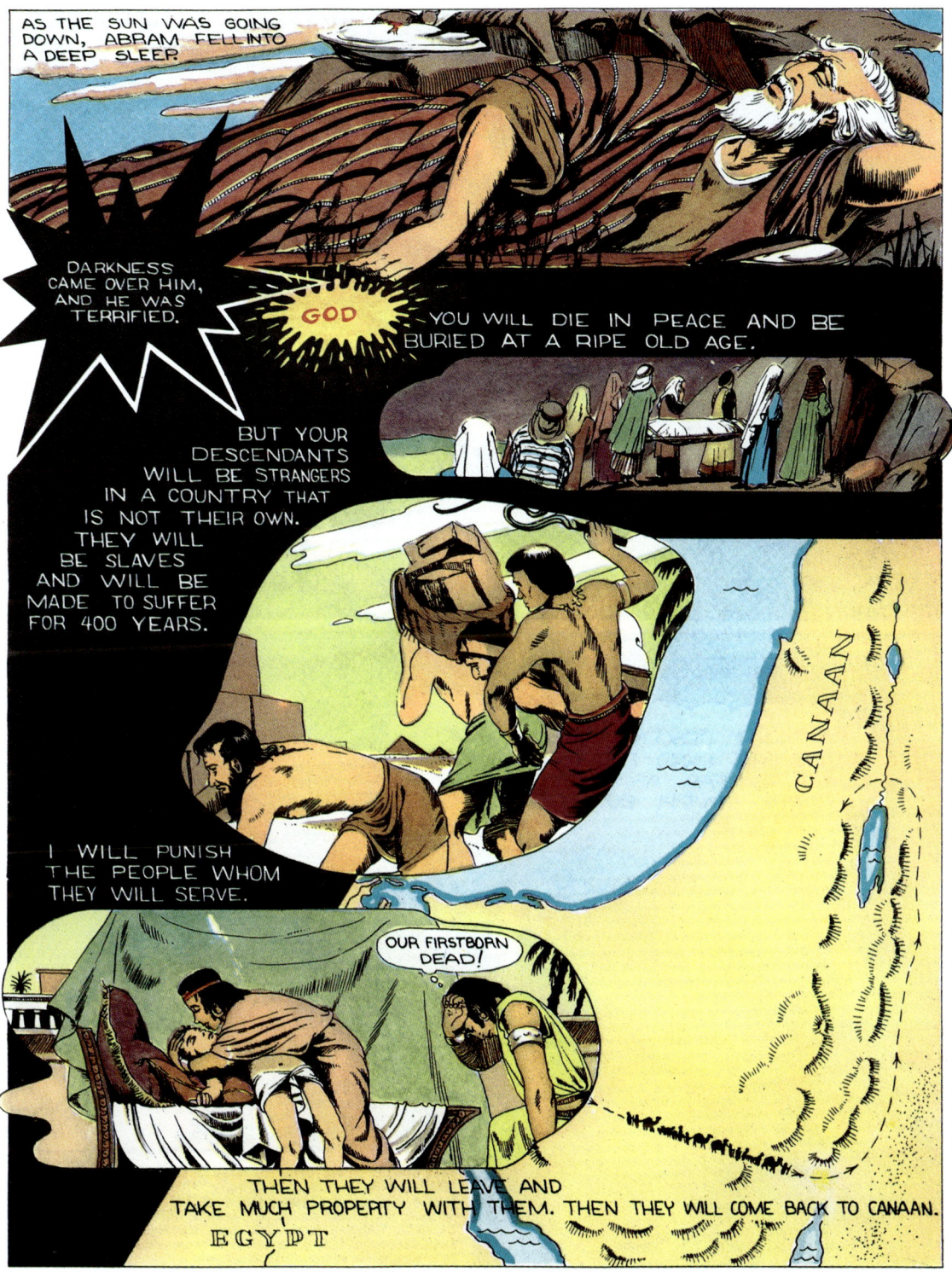

AFTER THE SUN HAD GONE DOWN AND IT WAS DARK, THERE WAS A SMOKING FIRE POT WITH A FLAME. IT PASSED BETWEEN THE PIECES OF MEAT.

ON THAT DAY THE LORD PROMISED ABRAM:

TO YOUR DESCENDANTS I HAVE GIVEN THIS LAND FROM THE RIVER OF EGYPT AS FAR AS THE GREAT RIVER, THE RIVER EUPHRATES.

Abraham and his wife Sarah are assured they will indeed have a son.

ABRAHAM TOOK SOUR MILK, SWEET MILK, AND THE CALF MEAT. HE SET THESE BEFORE HIS GUESTS. THEN HE WAITED ON THEM UNDER THE TREE WHILE THEY ATE.

WHERE IS YOUR WIFE SARAH?

THERE IN THE TENT.

I AM CERTAINLY COMING BACK TO YOU IN THE SPRING. THEN YOUR WIFE SARAH WILL HAVE A SON.

SARAH WAS LISTENING AT THE ENTRANCE OF THE TENT WHICH WAS BEHIND HIM.

Meanwhile Lot is living in the wicked city of Sodom. Two angels come to rescue Lot and his family.

THEN THEY STRUCK THE MEN WHO WERE IN FRONT OF THE DOOR OF THE HOUSE WITH BLINDNESS, BOTH YOUNG AND OLD, SO THAT THEY COULD NOT FIND THE DOOR.

DO YOU HAVE ANYONE HERE, A SON-IN-LAW, SONS, DAUGHTERS, OR ANYONE ELSE IN TOWN WHO BELONGS TO YOU? TAKE THEM AWAY FROM THIS PLACE, BECAUSE WE ARE GOING TO DESTROY IT. THE CRY THAT HAS COME TO THE LORD AGAINST THESE TOWNS IS SO GREAT THAT THE LORD HAS SENT US TO DESTROY THEM.

SO LOT WENT TO THE MEN WHO WERE GOING TO MARRY HIS DAUGHTERS.

GET UP AND LEAVE THIS PLACE BECAUSE THE LORD IS GOING TO DESTROY THE TOWN.

BUT THEY THOUGHT HE WAS JOKING.

WHEN THE MORNING DAWNED, THE ANGELS HURRIED LOT ALONG.

GET UP! TAKE YOUR WIFE AND YOUR TWO DAUGHTERS, WHO ARE WITH YOU; OTHERWISE YOU WILL BE DESTROYED WHEN THE TOWN IS PUNISHED.

Abraham gets into trouble again when he lies. He says he is Sarah's brother. God saves Abraham once more.

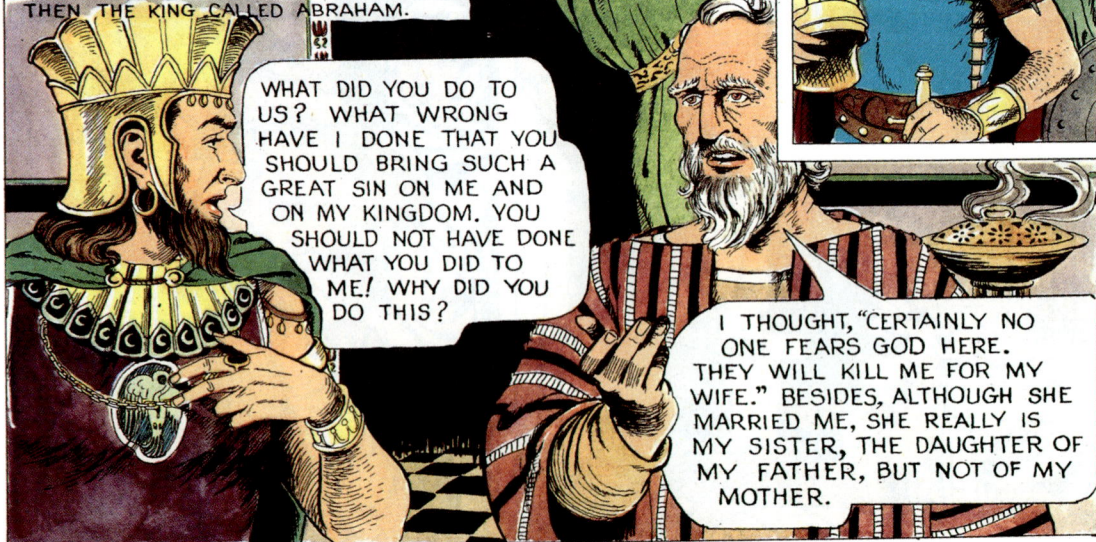

God now fulfills a promise He made to Abraham. He gives him two sons. One son, as God promised Abraham, is born to Sarah.

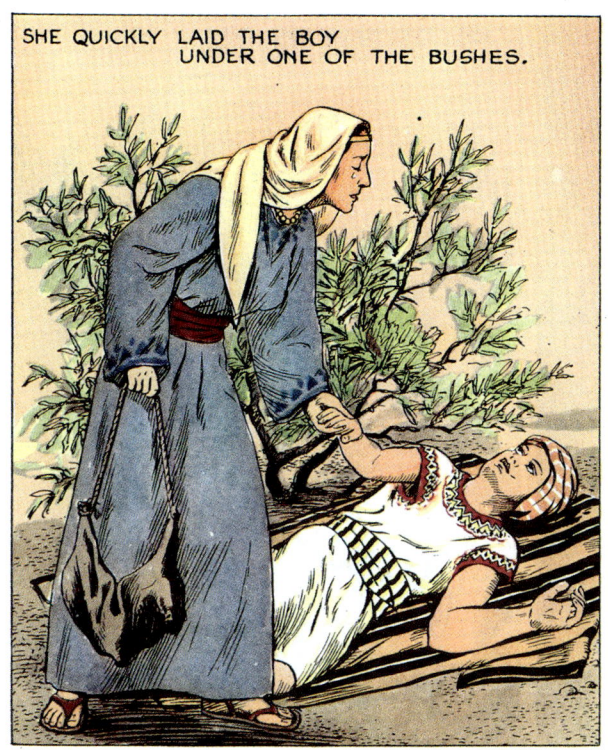

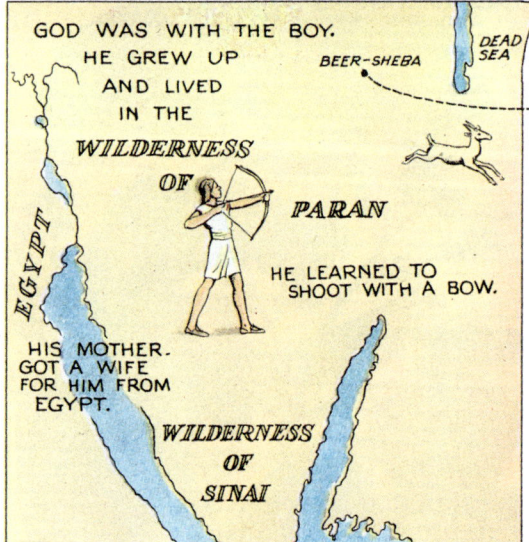

Abraham and Sarah had one son. God asks Abraham to sacrifice that son, Isaac. God wants to see if Abraham loves his son more than he loves God.

THE LORD: DON'T DO ANYTHING TO THE YOUNG MAN, BECAUSE I KNOW NOW THAT YOU FEAR GOD. YOU DID NOT REFUSE TO GIVE ME YOUR ONLY SON.

ABRAHAM LOOKED AROUND AND SAW A RAM BEHIND HIM, CAUGHT BY HIS HORNS IN A BUSH. SO ABRAHAM WENT AND GOT THE RAM AND SACRIFICED HIM INSTEAD OF HIS SON AS A BURNT OFFERING.

AGAIN THE ANGEL OF THE LORD CALLED FROM HEAVEN—

I SWEAR BY MYSELF: BECAUSE YOU DID NOT REFUSE TO GIVE ME YOUR ONLY SON, I WILL BLESS YOU RICHLY AND GIVE YOU—

MANY DESCENDANTS

LIKE THE STARS IN THE SKY

AND LIKE THE SAND ON THE SHORE OF THE SEA. IN YOUR DESCENDANT—

JESUS

ALL THE PEOPLE ON EARTH WILL BE BLESSED.

THEN ABRAHAM WENT BACK TO HIS SERVANTS, AND TOGETHER THEY WENT HOME TO BEER-SHEBA.

Abraham was willing to sacrifice his only son. Likewise, God sacrificed His one and only Son, Jesus, on the cross. By Jesus' sacrifice you are saved from the guilt of sin, the fear of death, and the power of the devil.

BIBLE STORIES in PICTURES
by W. F. BECK
ILLUSTRATED BY
RUTH W. ROGERS

The BIRTH of MOSES
EX. 2:1-10 ; ACTS 7:22

1527 B.C.

A MAN WHOSE NAME WAS **AMRAM** HAD A WIFE BY THE NAME OF **JOCHEBED**.

MIRIAM

AARON

WHILE THE KING OF EGYPT WAS TRYING TO KILL EVERY BOY THAT WAS BORN, JOCHEBED HAD A BABY BOY. SHE SAW THAT HE WAS A FINE BOY. SHE HID HIM FOR THREE MONTHS.

WHEN SHE COULDN'T HIDE HIM ANY LONGER, SHE GOT A BASKET, MADE OF PAPYRUS, SMEARED IT WITH ASPHALT AND PITCH...

AND LAID THE BOY IN IT.

Moses kills an Egyptian. He has to run away. God guides him. Moses becomes a shepherd.

SO MOSES GOT UP AND RESCUED THEM AND WATERED THEIR FLOCK.

THE DAUGHTERS CAME TO THEIR FATHER JETHRO.

"HOW DID YOU GET HERE SO EARLY TODAY?"

"AN EGYPTIAN RESCUED US FROM THE SHEPHERDS."

"HE ALSO DREW WATER FOR US AND WATERED THE FLOCK."

"WHERE IS HE? WHY DID YOU FAIL TO TAKE CARE OF THE MAN? ASK HIM TO COME AND EAT."

God now speaks to Moses out of a burning bush. God asks Moses to lead the Israelites out of Egypt. Will Moses obey God?

"I HAVE SEEN THE MISERY OF MY PEOPLE IN EGYPT AND HEARD THEM CRY UNDER THEIR OPPRESSORS. I KNOW HOW THEY ARE SUFFERING. I AM GOING DOWN TO DELIVER THEM FROM THE EGYPTIANS."

"NOW, COME, I WILL SEND YOU TO PHARAOH. BRING MY PEOPLE OUT OF EGYPT."

"WHO AM I THAT I SHOULD GO TO PHARAOH AND BRING ISRAEL OUT OF EGYPT?"

EGYPT

MOUNT SINAI

"I WILL CERTAINLY BE WITH YOU. THIS IS TO ASSURE YOU THAT I HAVE SENT YOU: WHEN YOU BRING THE PEOPLE OUT OF EGYPT, YOU WILL SERVE ME AT THIS MOUNTAIN."

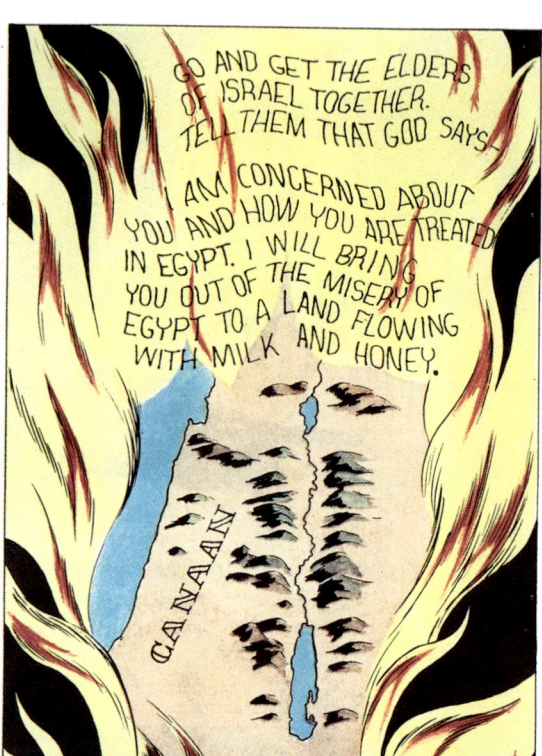

Moses makes all kinds of excuses. God shows Moses miracles Moses can perform. Finally Moses returns to Egypt.

Moses performs many miracles in Egypt. But Pharaoh does not let God's people go to the land of promise. Then God sends the angel of death. Learn what happens in the homes of the Egyptians and the homes of the Israelites.

MOSES TOOK THE BODY OF JOSEPH ALONG, BECAUSE LONG AGO JOSEPH HAD SAID TO THE OTHER ISRAELITES —

"GOD WILL SURELY COME TO HELP YOU. THEN TAKE MY BODY AWAY FROM HERE WITH YOU."

HE HAD THEM SWEAR THAT THEY WOULD DO IT.

NOW AFTER ISRAEL HAD BEEN IN EGYPT FOR 430 YEARS, THE LORD HAD ALL HIS PEOPLE MARCH OUT OF EGYPT. THERE WERE ABOUT 600,000 ON FOOT, COUNTING ONLY THE MEN AND NOT THE WOMEN AND CHILDREN.
ALSO A LARGE CROWD OF NON-ISRAELITES WENT UP WITH THEM AND MANY FLOCKS AND HERDS.

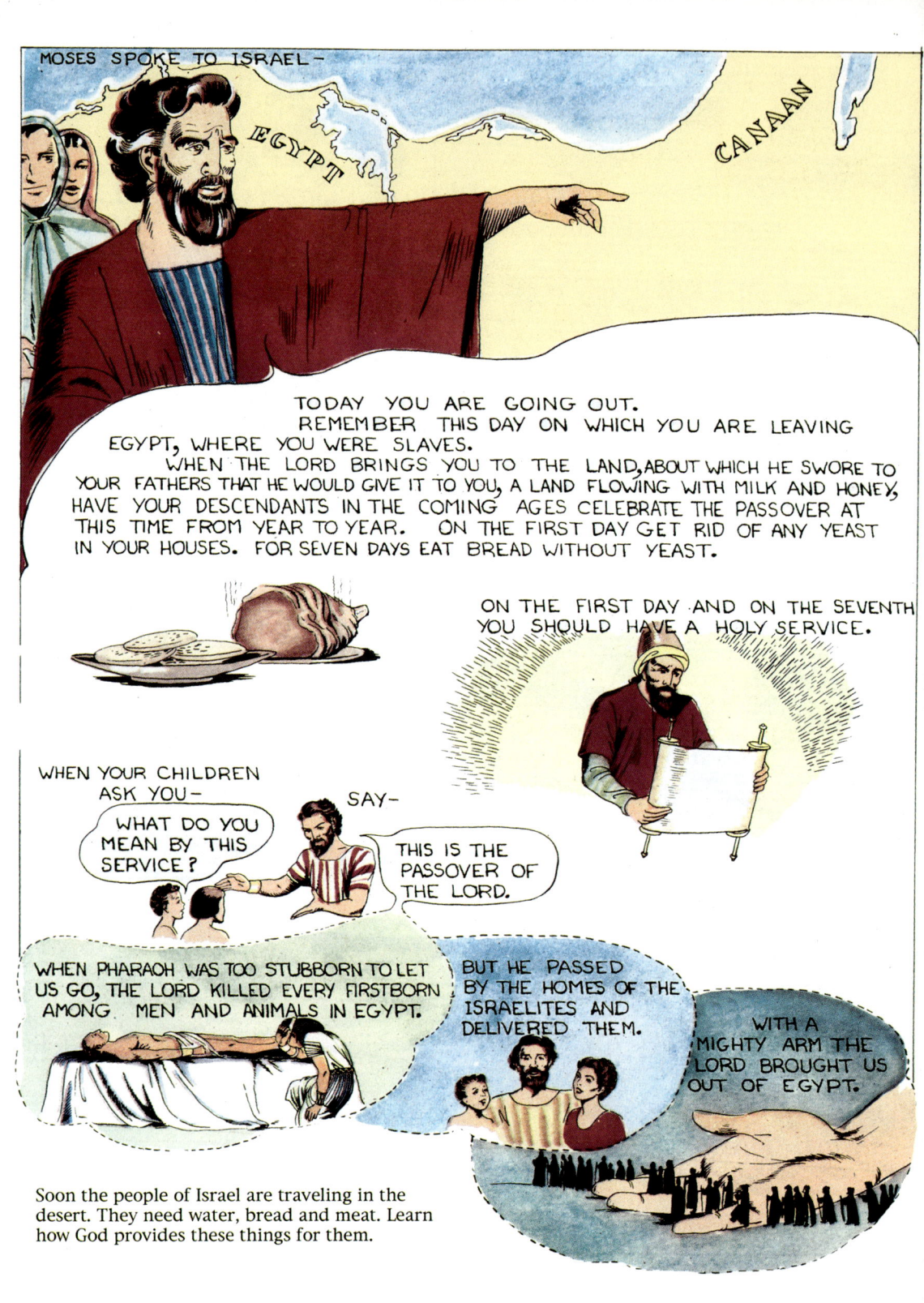

IN THE EVENING, QUAIL CAME UP AND COVERED THE CAMP.

AND IN THE MORNING A MIST WAS LYING AROUND THE CAMP. WHEN THE MIST LIFTED, THE GROUND OF THE WILDERNESS WAS COVERED WITH SOME FINE SCALY THINGS, AS FINE AS HOARFROST ON THE GROUND. THIS WAS THE "BREAD FROM HEAVEN."

God provides the Israelites with food to eat. God provides us with food also. We should be thankful for all God gives us.

Moses and the people of Israel reach Mount Sinai. Now read how God gives His people the Ten Commandments. These commandments affect your life today.

God's Ten Commandments have meaning in your life. Learn how and why you should fear, love and trust in God above everything and everyone.

God punishes the people because they sinned. But He does not destroy them. The people know Moses is God's representative.

The Lord now teaches the people of Israel how they should worship God.

BIBLE STORIES in PICTURES by W. F. BECK, illustrated by RUTH W. ROGERS

Worship the Lord

God said to Israel—

EVERY FIRSTBORN SON IS MINE.

INSTEAD OF EVERY FIRSTBORN SON I HAVE CHOSEN THE DESCENDANTS OF LEVI TO BE MINE. THEY BELONG TO ME AND SHOULD ALWAYS BE READY TO SERVE THE LORD. THEY SHOULD HELP AARON AND HIS SONS.

THE 10TH PART OF THE GRAIN OF THE LAND,

OF THE FRUIT OF THE TREES,

OF COWS AND SHEEP,

BELONGS TO THE LORD. I AM GIVING THIS 10TH PART TO THE DESCENDANTS OF LEVI FOR THE WORK THAT THEY ARE DOING.

WHEN THE LEVITES GET THE 10TH PART FROM THE ISRAELITES, THE LEVITES SHOULD SET ASIDE A 10TH OF THAT 10TH PART AS THE LORD'S SHARE AND GIVE IT TO AARON, THE PRIEST.

ALL MEN SHOULD VISIT THE LORD, THEIR GOD, THREE TIMES A YEAR AT THE PLACE WHICH HE CHOOSES—

FOR THE PASSOVER,

FOR THE HARVEST FESTIVAL,

AND FOR THE FESTIVAL OF BOOTHS.

WHEN YOU VISIT THE LORD, YOU SHOULD NOT COME EMPTY-HANDED. EVERYONE SHOULD GIVE WHAT HE CAN ACCORDING TO WHAT THE LORD HAS GIVEN HIM.

AFTER YOU HAVE GATHERED IN THE PRODUCTS OF THE FIELD, CELEBRATE THE LORD'S **FESTIVAL OF BOOTHS.** TAKE THE BOUGHS OF BEAUTIFUL TREES AND PALM BRANCHES, AND LIVE IN BOOTHS SO YOUR DESCENDANTS MAY LEARN HOW ISRAEL LIVED IN BOOTHS IN THE WILDERNESS. BE HAPPY BEFORE THE LORD FOR 7 DAYS, BECAUSE THE LORD BLESSES YOU IN EVERYTHING YOU DO.

CELEBRATE THE HARVEST FESTIVAL AS FOLLOWS—

GIVE AS LARGE A GIFT OF THE FIRST WHEAT WHICH YOU HARVEST AS YOU WANT TO GIVE.

FROM YOUR HOMES BRING TWO LOAVES OF BREAD, MADE OF 6½ QUARTS OF FINE FLOUR.

WITH THE BREAD BRING A SACRIFICE FOR THE LORD.

BE HAPPY BEFORE THE LORD WITH YOUR CHILDREN AND SERVANTS, WITH THE LEVITE, THE STRANGER, THE ORPHAN, AND THE WIDOW.

ON OCTOBER 1 BLOW THE HORN. HAVE A DAY OF REST WITH A HOLY MEETING, AND BRING SACRIFICES.

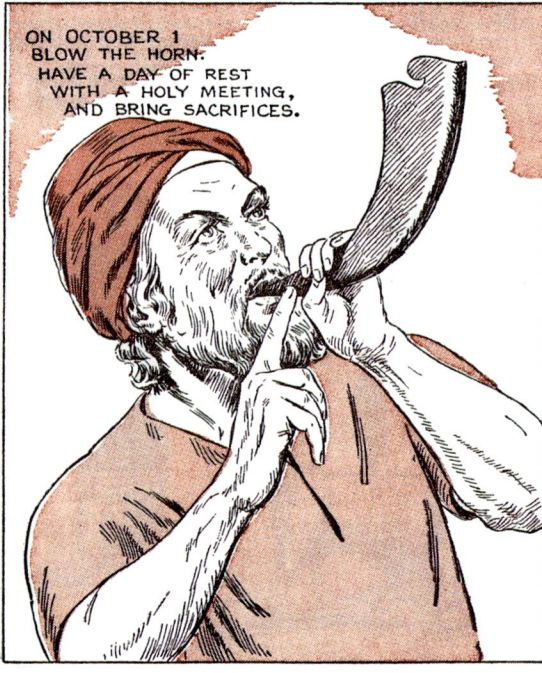

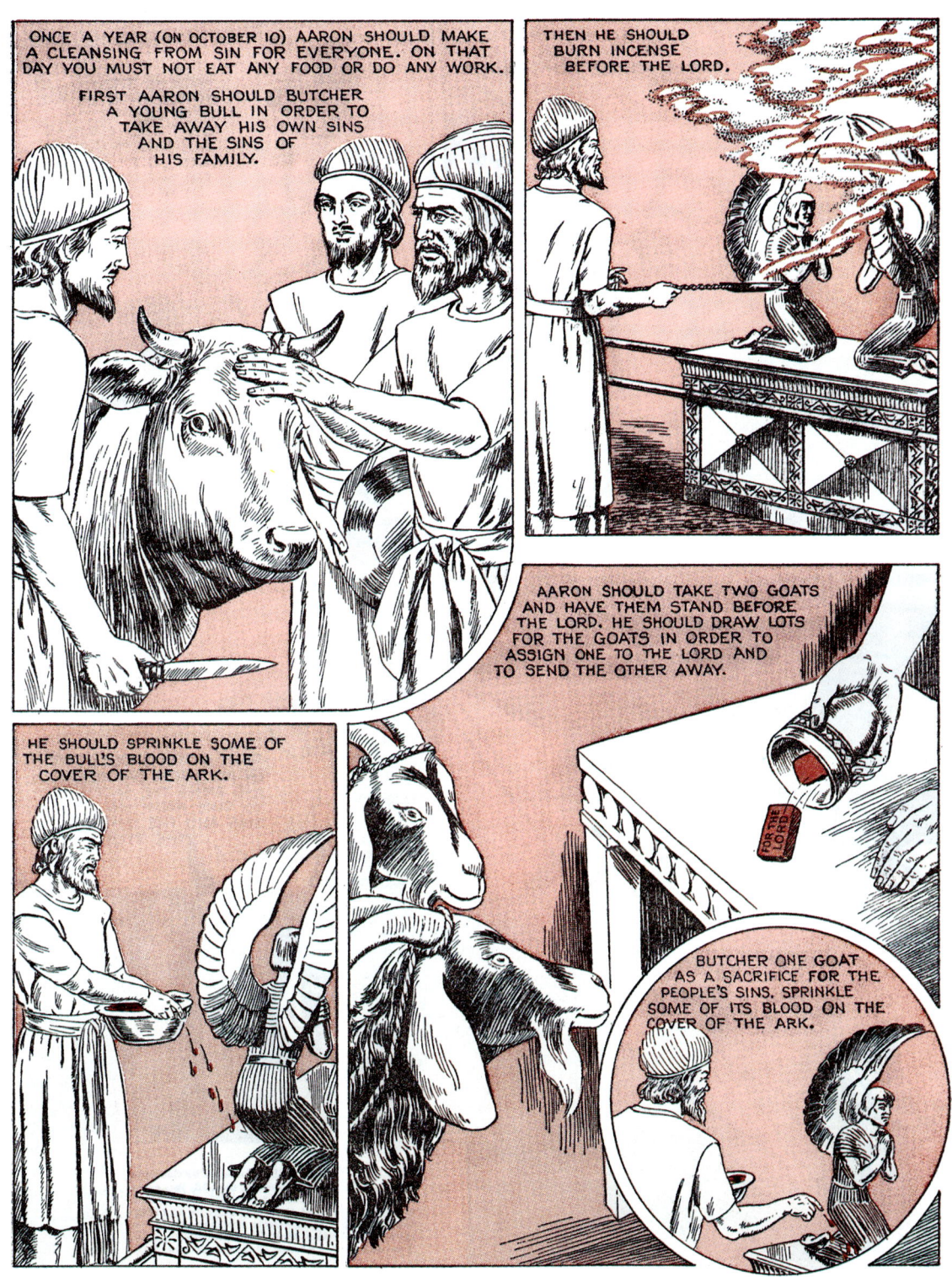

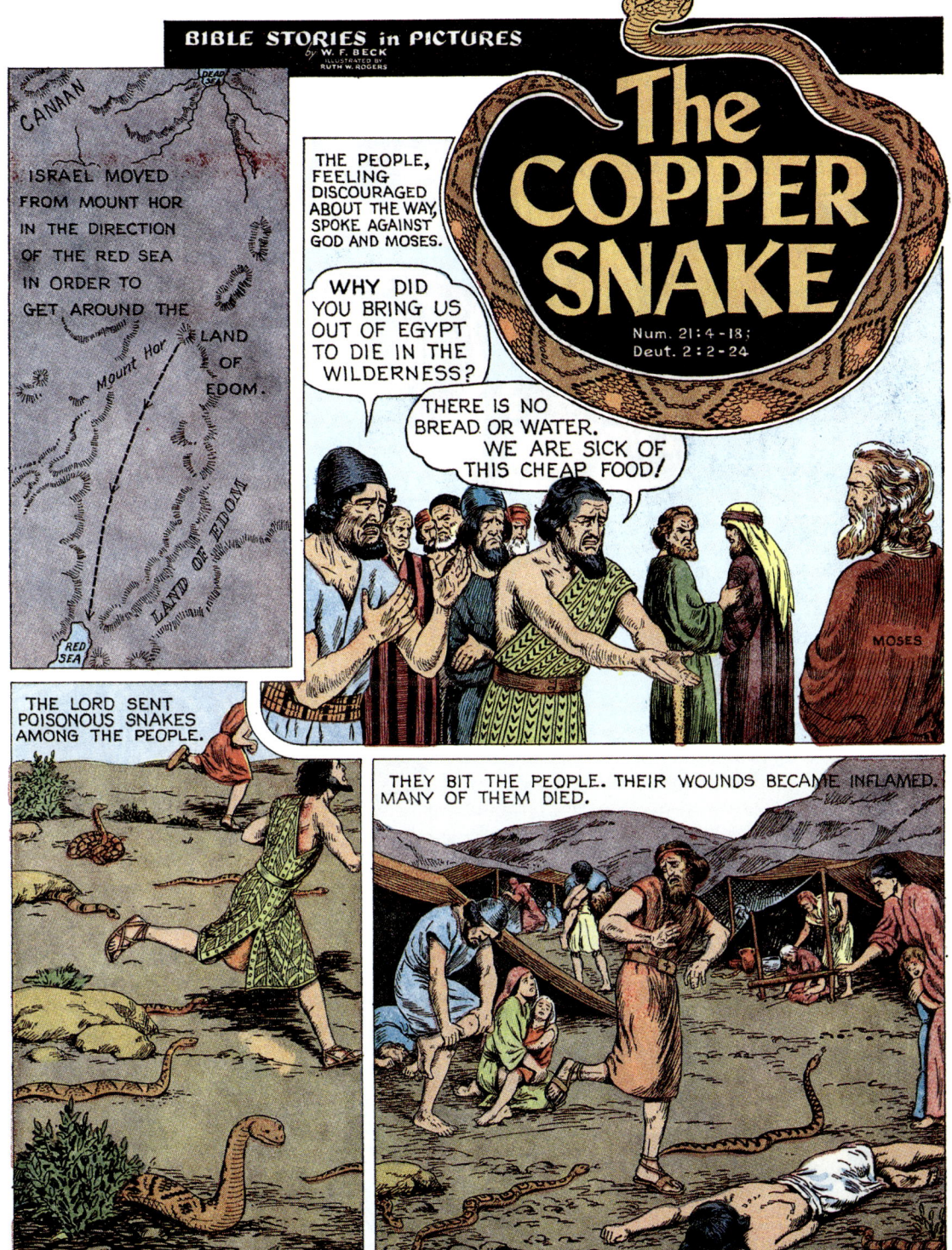

the Lord SAID TO MOSES

YOU HAVE GONE AROUND THESE HIGHLANDS LONG ENOUGH. TURN NORTH. INSTRUCT THE PEOPLE TO DO AS FOLLOWS: YOU ARE GOING THROUGH THE COUNTRY OF YOUR RELATIVES, THE PEOPLE OF EDOM. THEY ARE AFRAID OF YOU. BE VERY CAREFUL NOT TO START A WAR WITH THEM, BECAUSE I AM NOT GIVING YOU ANY OF THEIR LAND. BUY FOOD FROM THEM SO YOU CAN EAT. ALSO PAY THEM FOR THE WATER THAT YOU GET FROM THEM TO DRINK.

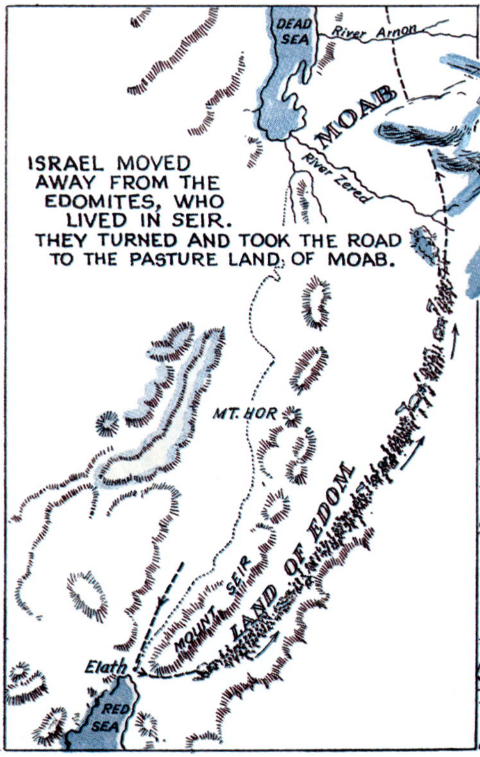

ISRAEL MOVED AWAY FROM THE EDOMITES, WHO LIVED IN SEIR. THEY TURNED AND TOOK THE ROAD TO THE PASTURE LAND OF MOAB.

DEAD SEA — River Arnon — MOAB — River Zered — MT. HOR — MOUNT SEIR — LAND OF EDOM — Elath — RED SEA

the Lord SAID TO MOSES

DON'T CAUSE MOAB ANY TROUBLE OR START A WAR WITH THEM, BECAUSE I AM NOT GIVING YOU ANY OF THEIR LAND. NOW START OUT AND CROSS THE VALLEY OF ZERED.

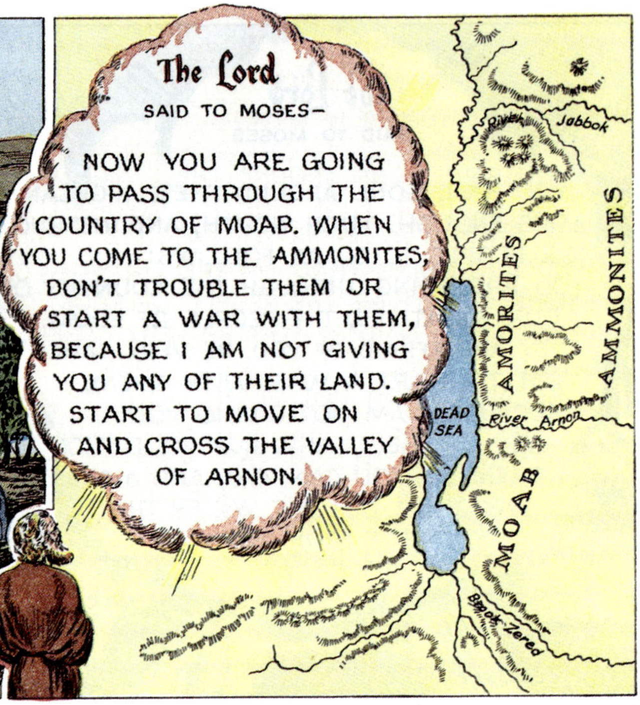

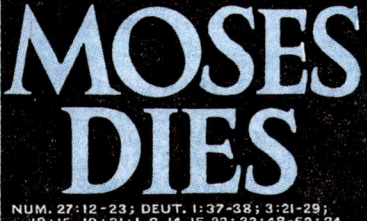

Moses is a great man of God. He led the people of Israel to the Promised Land of Canaan. Jesus, the Son of God, leads believers to the Promised Land of heaven.

Joshua now prepares the people to cross the Jordan River. God, by a miracle, makes it possible for the people to cross the river on dry land.

Joshua leads the people of Israel for many years. Before he dies, he asks the people to continue to serve the Lord.

ISRAEL CONTINUED TO FIGHT FOR THE LAND OF CANAAN. THEY WENT TO ATTACK BETHEL, AND THE LORD WAS WITH THEM.

BIBLE STORIES in PICTURES
by W. F. BECK
ILLUSTRATED BY RUTH W. ROGERS

DEBORAH
JUDGES 1-5

THEY SENT SPIES TO EXPLORE BETHEL. THE SPIES SAW A MAN COMING OUT OF THE CITY.

"PLEASE SHOW US A WAY INTO THE CITY. THEN WE WILL BE KIND TO YOU."

HE SHOWED THEM A WAY INTO THE CITY. THEY COMPLETELY DEFEATED THE CITY. BUT THEY LET THIS MAN AND HIS RELATIVES GO.

ISRAEL SERVED THE LORD DURING THE LIFETIME OF THE ELDERS WHO OUTLIVED JOSHUA AND HAD SEEN THE GREAT DEEDS WHICH THE LORD HAD DONE FOR ISRAEL.

"SO THE LORD SAVED ISRAEL FROM THE EGYPTIANS THAT DAY."

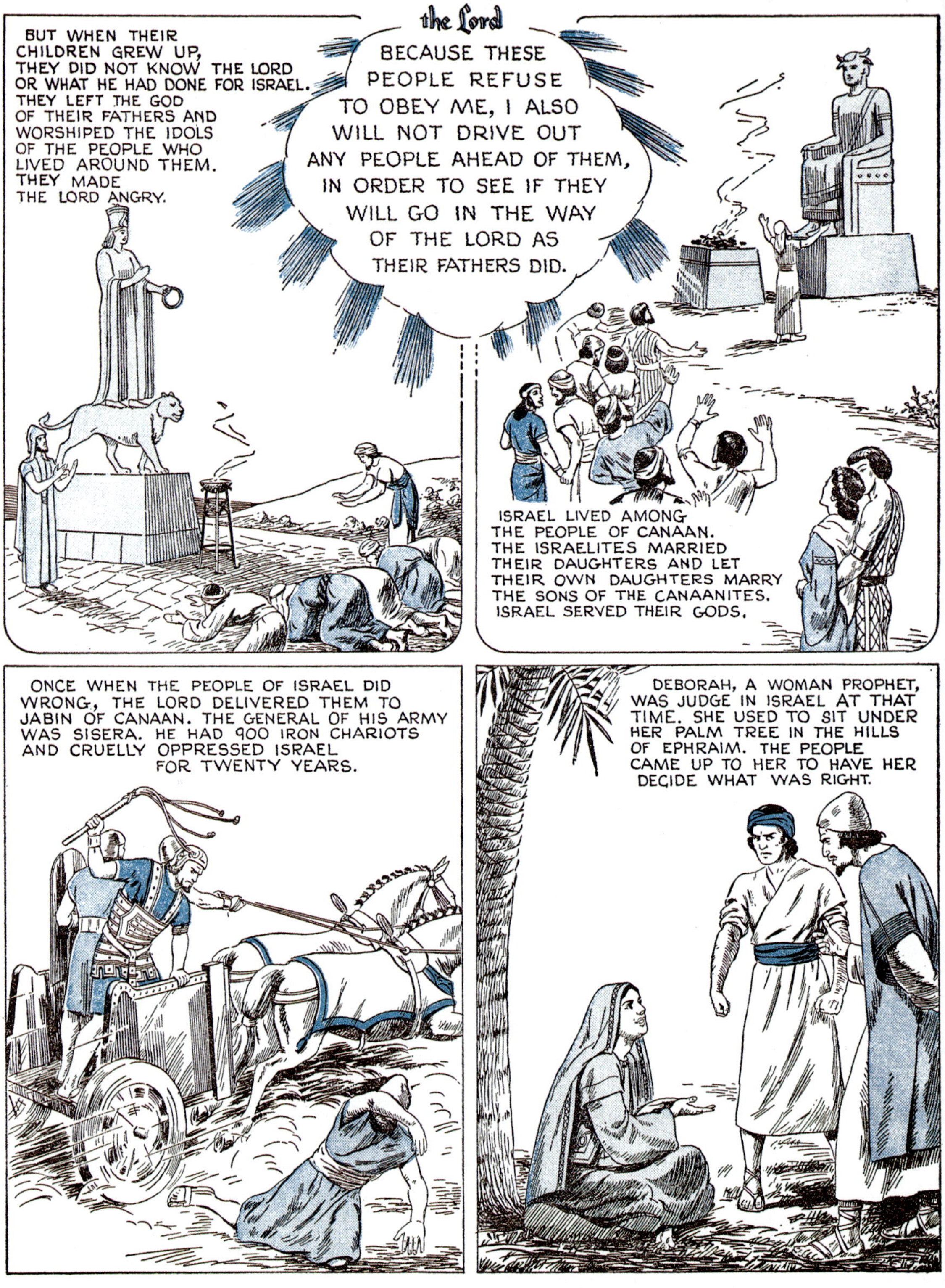

BUT WHEN THEIR CHILDREN GREW UP, THEY DID NOT KNOW THE LORD OR WHAT HE HAD DONE FOR ISRAEL. THEY LEFT THE GOD OF THEIR FATHERS AND WORSHIPED THE IDOLS OF THE PEOPLE WHO LIVED AROUND THEM. THEY MADE THE LORD ANGRY.

the Lord: BECAUSE THESE PEOPLE REFUSE TO OBEY ME, I ALSO WILL NOT DRIVE OUT ANY PEOPLE AHEAD OF THEM, IN ORDER TO SEE IF THEY WILL GO IN THE WAY OF THE LORD AS THEIR FATHERS DID.

ISRAEL LIVED AMONG THE PEOPLE OF CANAAN. THE ISRAELITES MARRIED THEIR DAUGHTERS AND LET THEIR OWN DAUGHTERS MARRY THE SONS OF THE CANAANITES. ISRAEL SERVED THEIR GODS.

ONCE WHEN THE PEOPLE OF ISRAEL DID WRONG, THE LORD DELIVERED THEM TO JABIN OF CANAAN. THE GENERAL OF HIS ARMY WAS SISERA. HE HAD 900 IRON CHARIOTS AND CRUELLY OPPRESSED ISRAEL FOR TWENTY YEARS.

DEBORAH, A WOMAN PROPHET, WAS JUDGE IN ISRAEL AT THAT TIME. SHE USED TO SIT UNDER HER PALM TREE IN THE HILLS OF EPHRAIM. THE PEOPLE CAME UP TO HER TO HAVE HER DECIDE WHAT WAS RIGHT.

That Day Deborah and Barak Sang a Song:

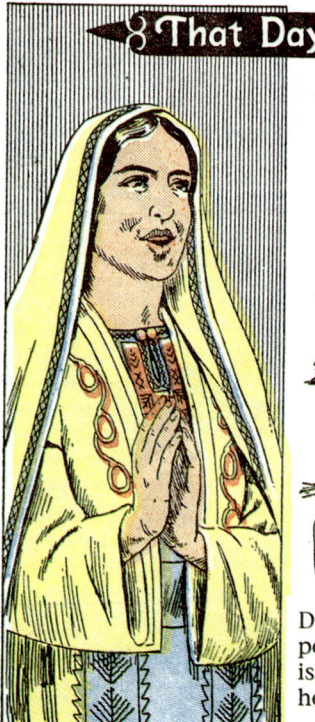

Praise the Lord: He has done a righteous thing! The stars fought from heaven; they fought from their highways with Sisera.

The Kishon River swept them away— may all your enemies, Lord, perish like that!

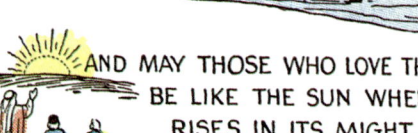

And may those who love the Lord be like the sun when it rises in its might.

During the days of the Judges, there were many people who loved and served God. Among them is a woman named Ruth. She is very faithful to her mother-in-law Naomi.

SHE TOOK IT AND WENT INTO THE TOWN. HER MOTHER-IN-LAW SAW WHAT SHE HAD GLEANED. RUTH ALSO BROUGHT OUT WHAT HAD BEEN LEFT OVER AFTER SHE HAD EATEN ENOUGH. SHE GAVE IT TO NAOMI.

WHERE DID YOU GLEAN TODAY, AND WHERE DID YOU WORK? BLESSED BE THE MAN WHO ATTENDED TO YOU.

I WORKED TODAY WITH A MAN WHOSE NAME IS BOAZ.

THE LORD, WHO HAS NOT STOPPED BEING KIND TO THE LIVING AND THE DEAD, BLESS HIM!

HE ALSO TOLD ME, "STAY NEAR MY SERVANTS UNTIL THEY HAVE HARVESTED ALL MY GRAIN."

IT IS BEST, MY DAUGHTER, THAT YOU GO OUT WITH HIS WOMEN. THEN YOU WILL NOT BE IN A STRANGE FIELD WHERE PEOPLE MAY MISTREAT YOU.

RUTH STAYED WITH THE WOMEN OF BOAZ. SHE GLEANED UNTIL ALL THE BARLEY AND THE WHEAT HAD BEEN HARVESTED. BUT SHE LIVED WITH HER MOTHER-IN-LAW.

God blesses Ruth through Boaz. Now Boaz marries Ruth. They have a son. King David and later Jesus come from this son.

Many years pass. A woman without children prays that she might have a son. A son named Samuel is born to her. He will serve the Lord faithfully.

Samuel continues to serve the Lord. The people of Israel are not satisfied with the Judges who rule. They want a king.

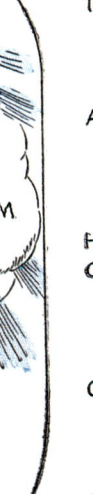

Saul remains king for forty years. But Saul becomes evil. God is not pleased with Saul. God then chooses David, a shepherd, to be the next king.

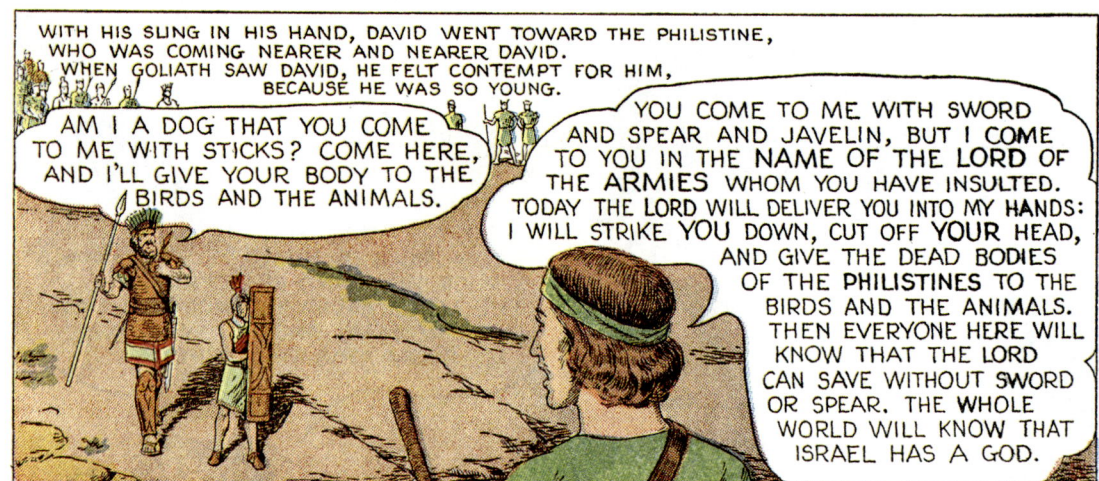

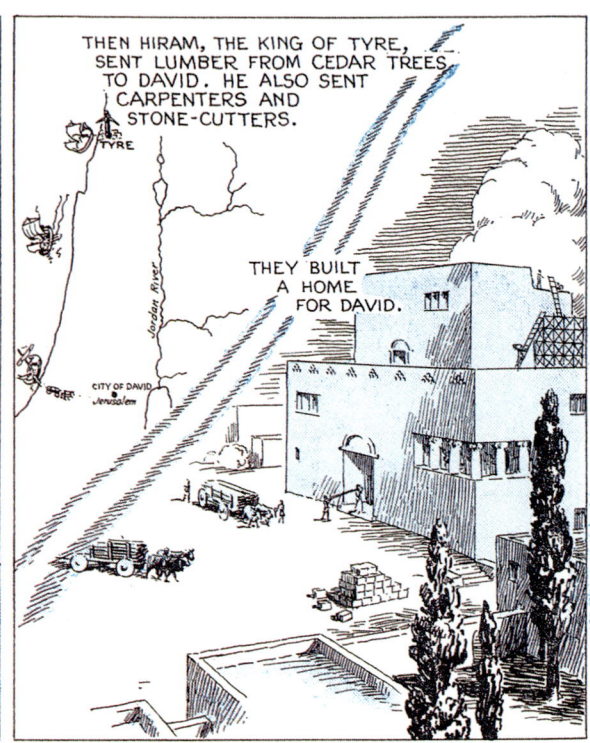

David rules as king for forty years.
His son, Solomon, then becomes king.
Solomon is a very wise king.

New Testament

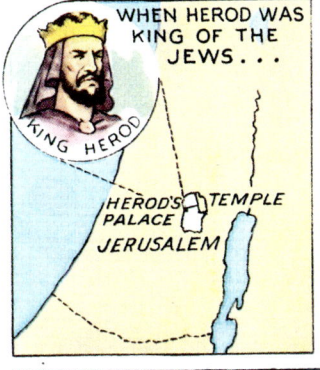

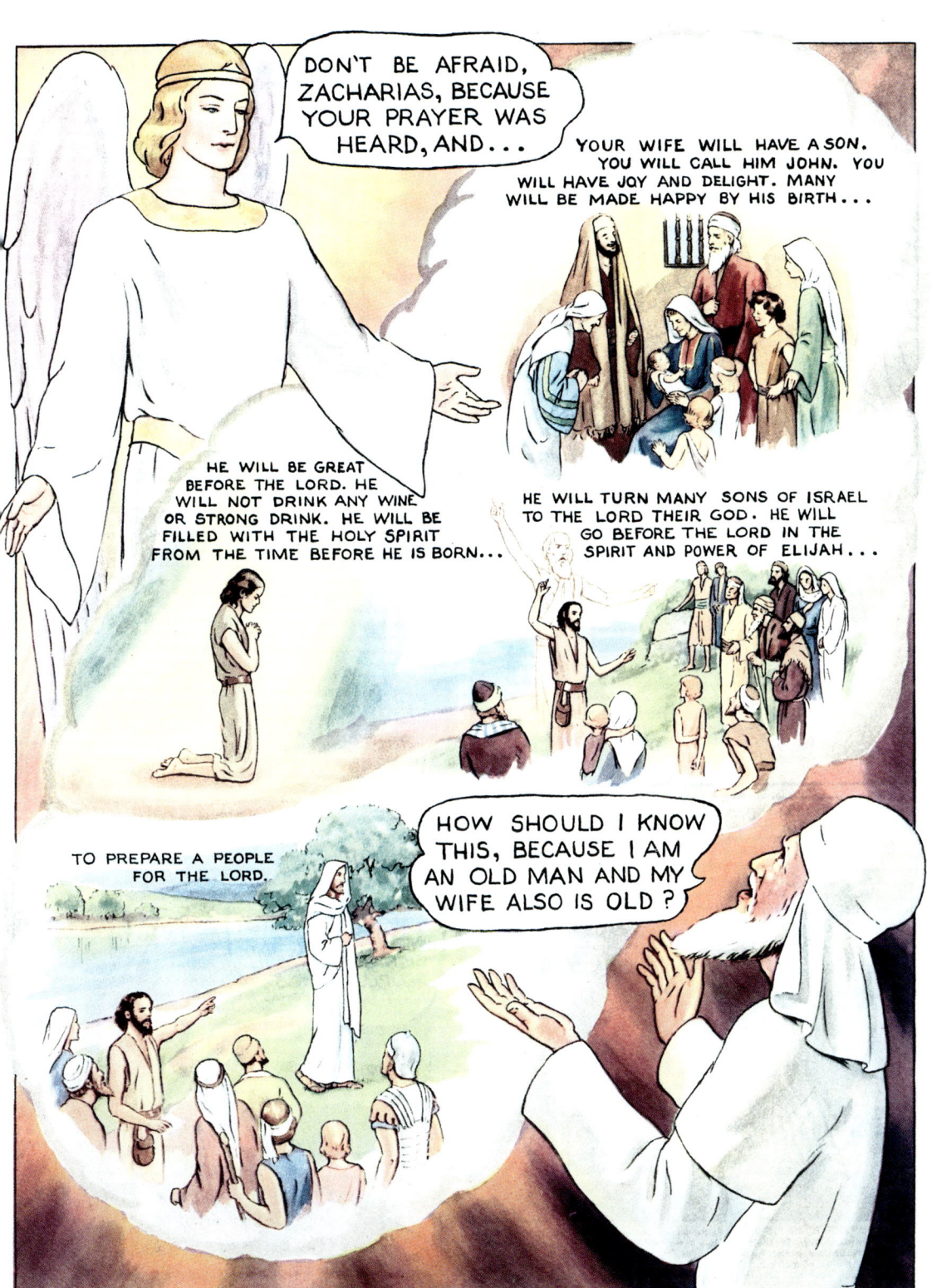

In the next story read about Mary.
She is the mother of your Savior.

*Elizabeth had felt it was a disgrace not to have a child.

MARY VISITS ELIZABETH
LUKE 1:39-56
Nazareth–Hill Country of Judea
March – June, 5 B.C.

My soul praises the Lord,
And my spirit delights in God, my Savior,
  For He looked at the lowliness of His servant,
  And from now on all people will call me blessed.

For He did great things to me—
  He who is mighty,
  And whose name is holy,
  And whose mercy is always with
      those who fear Him.

He did mighty deeds with His arm:
He scattered those who think
    proudly in their hearts.

  He put down the mighty
    from their thrones
        And lifted up the lowly.
He filled the hungry with good things,
  And the rich He sent away empty.

He helped His servant Israel
    Because He would remember

His Mercy

Which He promised to our fathers
And which He gave to Abraham,
  and to His children FOREVER.

Soon John, the son of Zacharias and Elizabeth, is to be born.

MARY STAYED WITH HER ABOUT THREE MONTHS, AND THEN WENT BACK TO HER HOME.

It is now time for Jesus to be born.

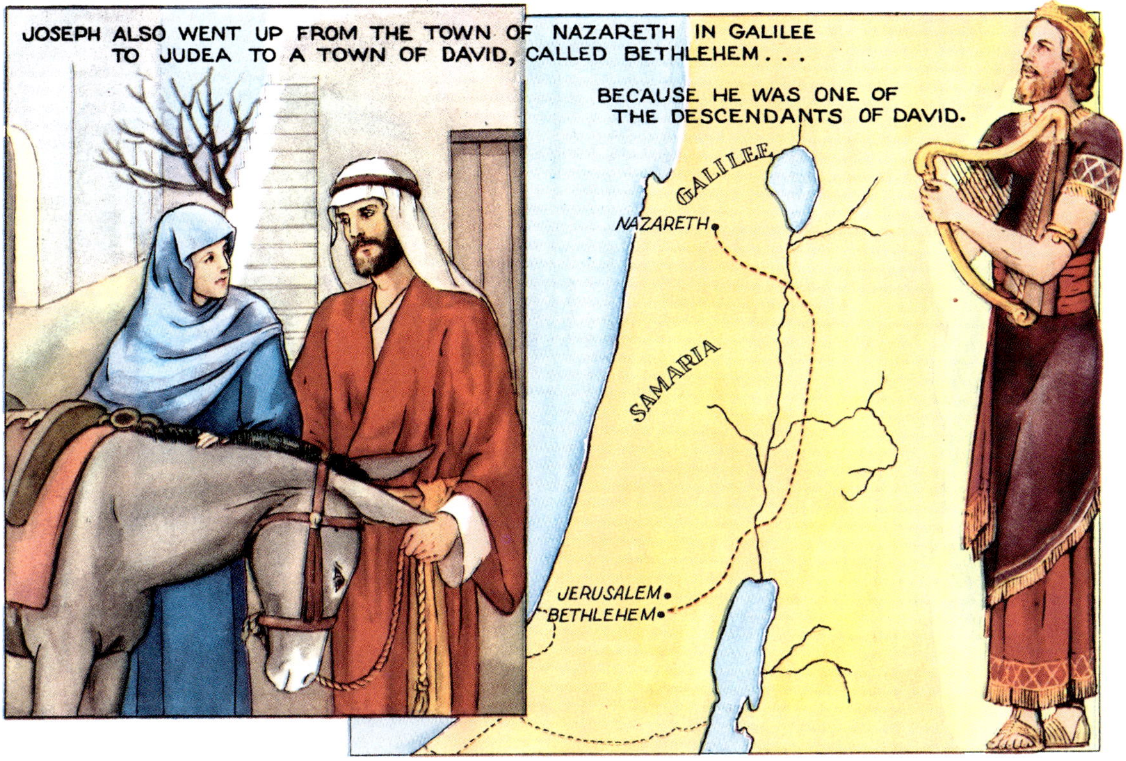

JOSEPH ALSO WENT UP FROM THE TOWN OF NAZARETH IN GALILEE TO JUDEA TO A TOWN OF DAVID, CALLED BETHLEHEM...

BECAUSE HE WAS ONE OF THE DESCENDANTS OF DAVID.

TO REGISTER WITH MARY, HIS WIFE, WHO WAS GOING TO HAVE A CHILD.

An angel from God tells shepherds Jesus is born.

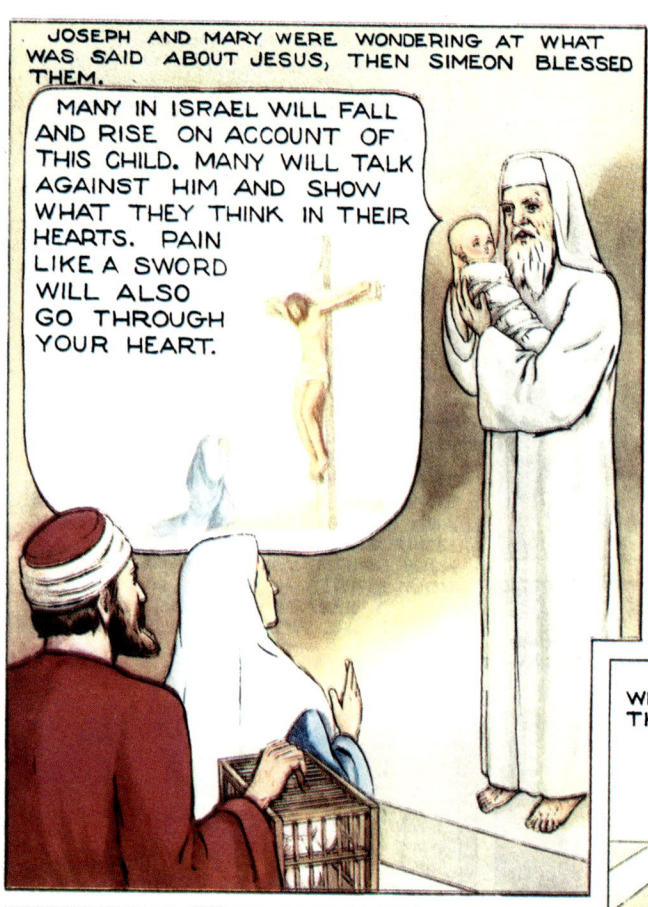

Others, non-Jews, come to worship Jesus.

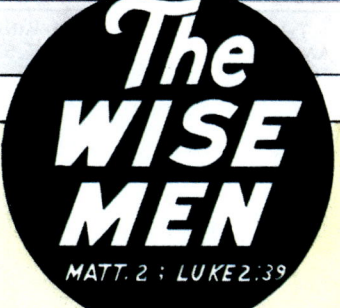

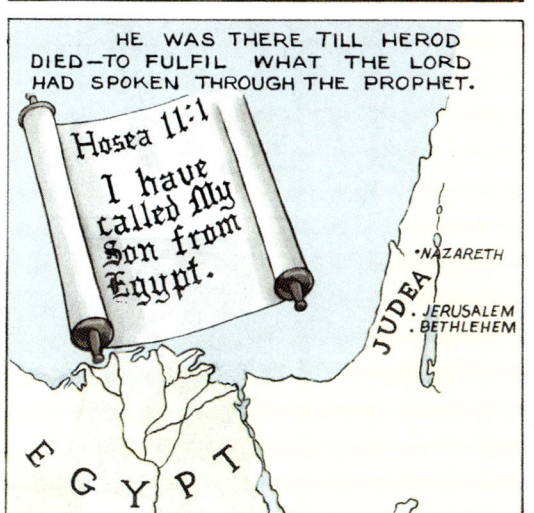

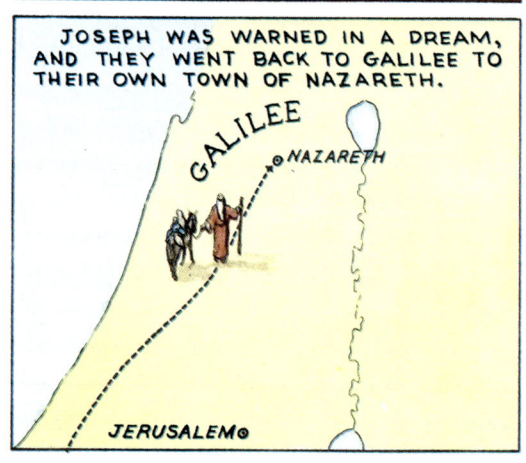

Now read about Jesus as a boy.

BIBLE STORIES in PICTURES
by W. F. BECK
ILLUSTRATED BY RUTH W. ROGERS

JESUS at TWELVE
LUKE 2:40-52

Nazareth, Jerusalem April 8-14, 8 A.D.

THE LITTLE CHILD GREW. HE BECAME STRONG AND WISE. THE LOVE OF GOD WAS WITH HIM.

EVERY YEAR HIS PARENTS WOULD GO UP TO JERUSALEM TO CELEBRATE THE PASSOVER.

HEROD'S PALACE

TEMPLE

WHEN HE WAS 12 YEARS OLD, THEY WENT UP AS THEY USED TO DO...

FOR THE FESTIVAL.

Read more about the teachings of Jesus, his death and rising from the dead.

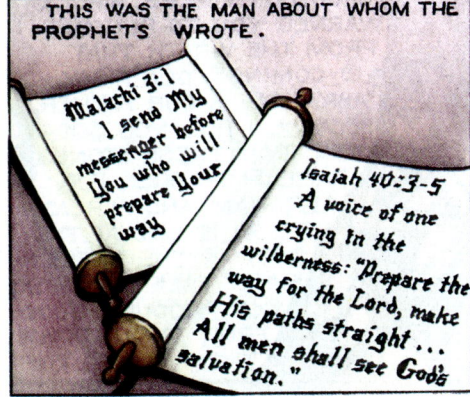

IS THIS MAN CHRIST?

ONE WHO IS MIGHTIER THAN I IS COMING AFTER ME. I AM NOT FIT TO STOOP DOWN AND UNTIE THE STRAP OF HIS SHOES. I BAPTIZE YOU WITH WATER. HE WILL BAPTIZE YOU WITH THE HOLY SPIRIT AND WITH FIRE.

GALILEE

SEA OF GALILEE

WHEN JESUS WAS ABOUT 30 YEARS OLD, HE WENT FROM NAZARETH IN GALILEE TO THE JORDAN TO BE BAPTIZED BY JOHN.

JERICHO

JORDAN RIVER

BETHANY

JESUS LEAVES HIS MOTHER.

Jesus is baptized. After the baptism He begins preaching and teaching. He shows He is the Son of God by His wonderful words and deeds.

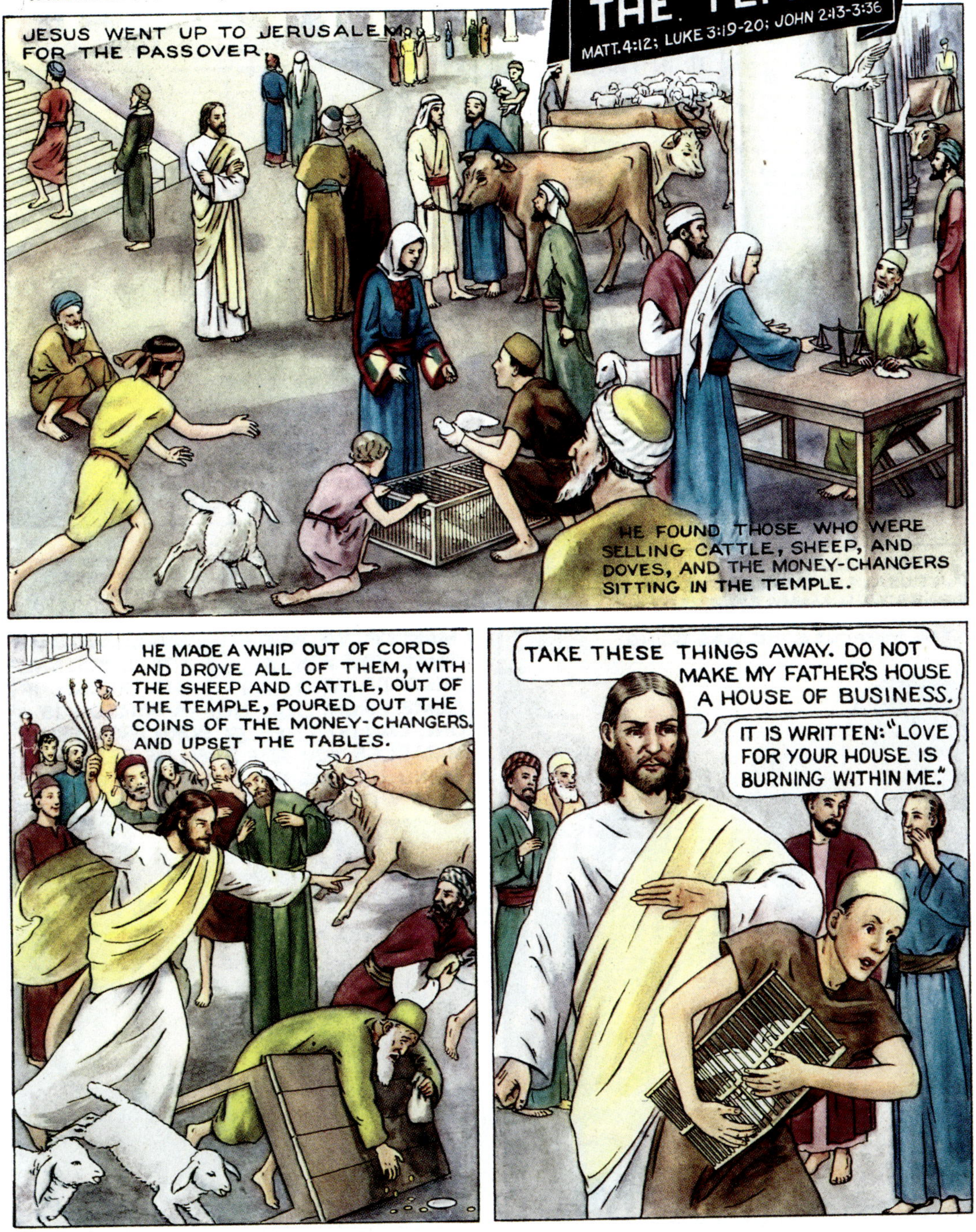

"BY WHAT MIRACLE CAN YOU SHOW US THAT YOU HAVE A RIGHT TO DO THIS?"

"DESTROY THIS TEMPLE, AND I WILL RAISE IT IN THREE DAYS."

"IT TOOK FORTY-SIX YEARS TO BUILD THIS TEMPLE, AND YOU ARE GOING TO RAISE IT IN THREE DAYS."

BY "THE TEMPLE" HE MEANT HIS OWN BODY. AFTER HE HAD RISEN FROM THE DEAD, HIS DISCIPLES REMEMBERED THAT HE HAD SAID THIS; AND THEY BELIEVED WHAT JESUS HAD SAID.

NICODEMUS

WHILE JESUS WAS IN JERUSALEM DURING THE PASSOVER, MANY BELIEVED IN HIM, BECAUSE THEY SAW THE MIRACLES HE WAS DOING.

NICODEMUS, A PHARISEE AND A RULER OF THE JEWS, CAME TO JESUS BY NIGHT.

"MASTER, WE KNOW THAT YOU ARE A TEACHER WHO HAS COME FROM GOD. NO ONE CAN DO THE MIRACLES YOU ARE DOING UNLESS GOD IS WITH HIM."

"I TELL YOU THE TRUTH: ONLY IF A PERSON IS BORN FROM ABOVE CAN HE SEE THE KINGDOM OF GOD."

Jesus not only speaks to men like Nicodemus, but also to women. He tells them He is the promised Savior who was to come into the world.

Jesus goes on to heal a sick boy. He speaks of Himself as the great prophet who is to come into the world.

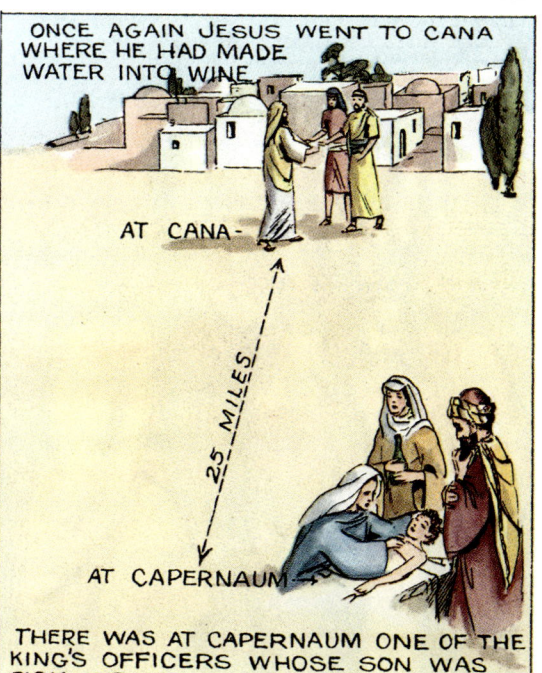

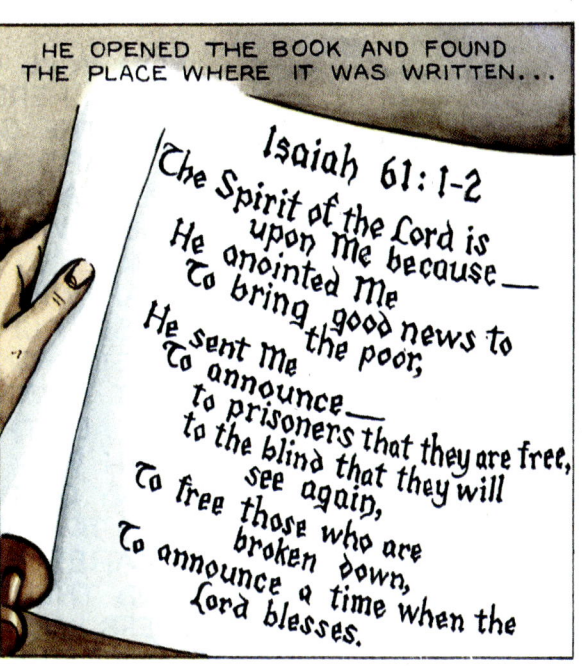

YOU WILL CERTAINLY TELL ME, "DO HERE IN YOUR HOME TOWN THE GREAT THINGS WE HEARD YOU DID IN CAPERNAUM."

THERE WERE MANY WIDOWS IN ISRAEL IN THE DAYS OF ELIJAH WHEN THE SKY WAS SHUT UP THREE YEARS AND SIX MONTHS, AND A GREAT FAMINE CAME OVER ALL THE LAND. YET ELIJAH WAS NOT SENT TO ANY OF THEM BUT ONLY TO THE WIDOW AT ZAREPHATH IN SIDON. THERE WERE MANY LEPERS IN ISRAEL AT THE TIME OF THE PROPHET ELISHA. NONE OF THEM WAS CLEANSED EXCEPT NAAMAN, THE SYRIAN.

(JESUS TELLS THEM: ELISHA AND ELIJAH HELPED PEOPLE OUTSIDE OF GALILEE. IN THE SAME WAY JESUS MAY DO HIS MIRACLES IN OTHER PLACES, BUT NOT IN NAZARETH.)

ALL IN THE SYNAGOG BECAME VERY ANGRY, GOT UP, PUT HIM OUT OF THE TOWN, AND TOOK HIM TO A BROW OF THE HILL ON WHICH THEIR TOWN WAS BUILT, TO HURL HIM DOWN THE CLIFF.

BUT HE PASSED THROUGH THE MIDDLE OF THEM AND WENT HIS WAY.

Jesus leaves His home town. He calls some of His disciples to follow Him. He heals the sick. He preaches good news.

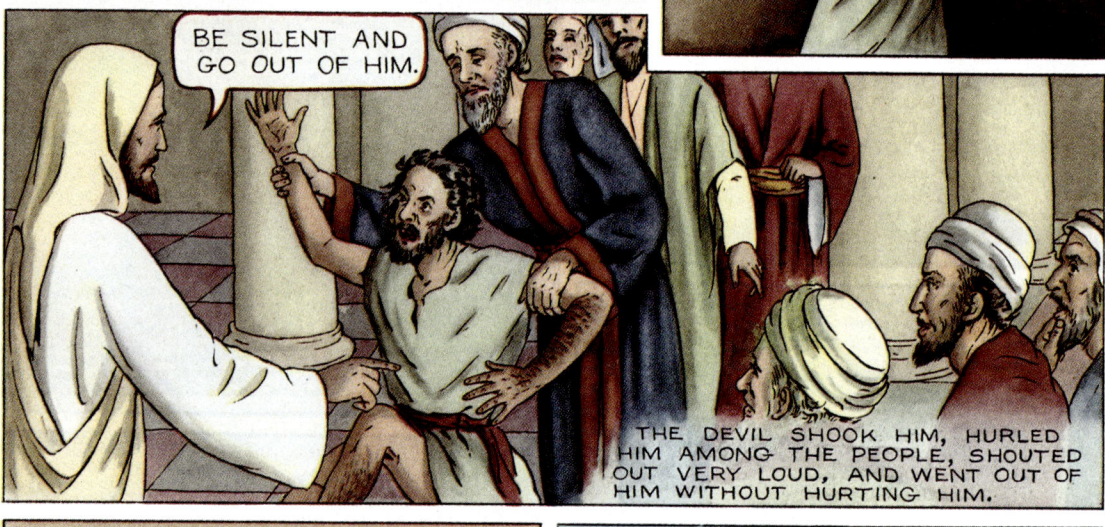

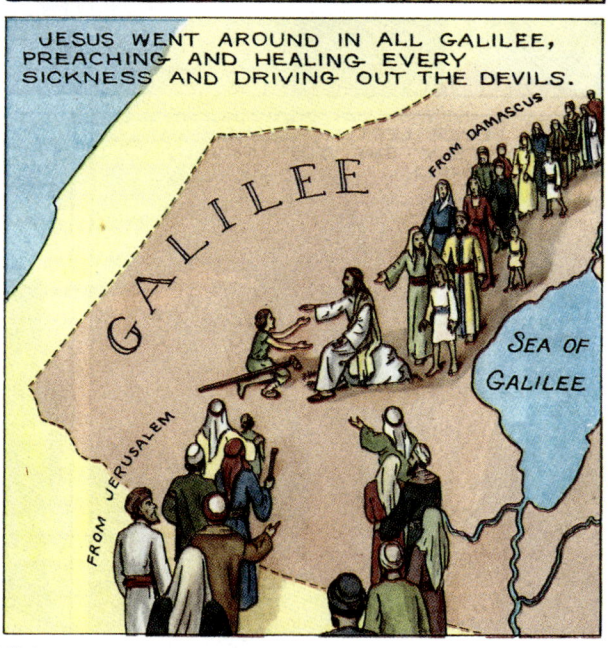

THE PROPHET ISAIAH HAD SAID,
"THE PEOPLE WHO WERE SITTING IN DARKNESS
SAW A GREAT LIGHT;
ON THOSE WHO SAT IN THE LAND OF THE SHADOW OF DEATH
A LIGHT HAS RISEN."

Jesus now forgives a man his sins. Then He heals the man to show He has that power also. The people are amazed and praise God.

BIBLE STORIES in PICTURES
by W. F. BECK
ILLUSTRATED BY RUTH W. ROGERS

JESUS FORGIVES SINS
MATT. 9:1-17; MARK 2:1-22; LUKE 5:17-39

Capernaum — Early in 28 A.D.

AFTER SOME DAYS JESUS CAME AGAIN TO HIS OWN TOWN OF CAPERNAUM.

ONE DAY SO MANY CAME TOGETHER THAT THERE WAS NO ROOM EVEN IN FRONT OF THE DOOR. HE WAS SPEAKING THE WORD OF GOD TO THEM.

HE IS HOME.

PHARISEES AND TEACHERS OF THE LAW, WHO HAD COME FROM EVERY VILLAGE IN GALILEE AND JUDEA AND FROM JERUSALEM WERE SITTING THERE.

Jesus shows He is the Son of God by yet another miracle. Everyone should honor Jesus as God.

Jesus not only heals the sick, but He also raises the dead. The great power of Jesus shows us He is indeed the Son of God.

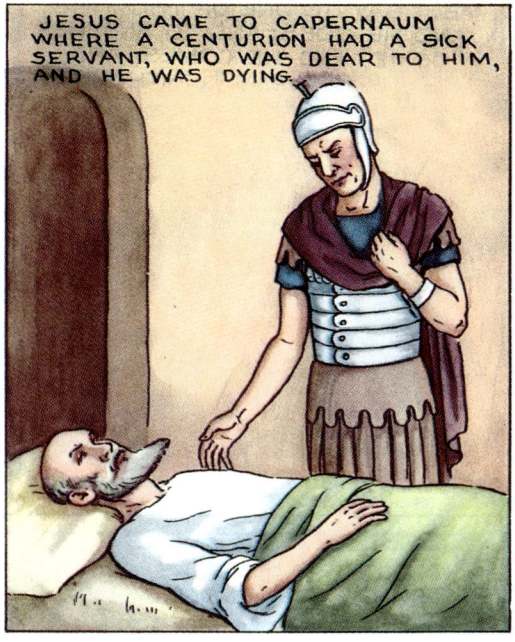

In days of trouble we can go to Jesus for help. He now shows Himself as God's Son in a most wonderful way.

By believing in Jesus He becomes our Savior. He came into the world to save all people.

By His teaching and miracles Jesus shows He is the Son of God. By His death and rising to life again, He also shows that He is our Savior.

Judas, one of Jesus' twelve disciples, comes with a crowd of Jesus' enemies. Judas will betray Jesus.

BIBLE STORIES in PICTURES
by W. F. BECK
ILLUSTRATED BY RUTH W. ROGERS

JUDAS BETRAYS JESUS

MATT. 26:47-57　MARK 14:43-54
LUKE 22:47-54　JOHN 18:2-14

Gethsemane　　THURSDAY NIGHT, APRIL 6-7

JUDAS, ONE OF THE TWELVE, WHO WAS BETRAYING JESUS, ALSO KNEW THE PLACE, BECAUSE JESUS AND HIS DISCIPLES HAD OFTEN COME TOGETHER THERE.

SO JUDAS TOOK THE BAND OF SOLDIERS AND SERVANTS OF THE HIGH PRIESTS AND PHARISEES. THE TRAITOR AGREED WITH THEM ON A SIGN.

"HE WHOM I KISS WILL BE THE ONE. ARREST HIM, TAKE HIM AWAY, DON'T LET HIM ESCAPE."

WHILE JESUS WAS STILL SPEAKING, JUDAS CAME THERE. WITH HIM WAS A LARGE CROWD FROM THE HIGH PRIESTS, SCRIBES, AND ELDERS OF THE PEOPLE, WITH LANTERNS AND TORCHES, SWORDS AND CLUBS.

JESUS KNEW ALL THAT WAS GOING TO HAPPEN TO HIM. SO HE WENT OUT—

"WHOM ARE YOU LOOKING FOR?"

"JESUS OF NAZARETH."

Jesus is now in the hands of His enemies. The soldiers take Jesus to the Jewish religious court.

BIBLE STORIES in PICTURES
by W. F. BECK
ILLUSTRATED BY RUTH W. ROGERS

BEFORE ANNAS AND CAIAPHAS

MATT. 26:57-68 MARK 14:53-65
LUKE 22:54-55:63-65 JOHN 18:15-25

Jerusalem   1-6 A.M. FRIDAY

SIMON PETER AND ANOTHER DISCIPLE FOLLOWED JESUS AT A DISTANCE.

THIS OTHER DISCIPLE WAS KNOWN TO THE HIGH PRIEST. HE WENT IN WITH JESUS INTO THE HIGH PRIEST'S COURTYARD, WHILE PETER STOOD OUTSIDE AT THE DOOR.

SO THE OTHER DISCIPLE WENT OUTSIDE AND SPOKE TO THE WOMAN WHO WATCHED THE DOOR.

HE BROUGHT PETER INTO THE COURTYARD OF THE HIGH PRIEST.
THE SERVANTS AND THE GUARDS WHO WERE STANDING AROUND HAD LIT A FIRE IN THE MIDDLE OF THE COURTYARD. THEY HAD MADE A HEAP OF BURNING COALS, BECAUSE IT WAS COLD.

As a prisoner, Jesus was sent to Pontius Pilate. Pilate was the Roman governor. After a short trial, Pilate sent Jesus to the Jewish King Herod.

Seeking the sympathy of the Jewish people, Pilate has Jesus whipped and mocked. Yet, the crowd cries out to crucify Jesus.

BIBLE STORIES in PICTURES
by W. F. BECK — ILLUSTRATED BY RUTH W. ROGERS

"SEE THE MAN"

MATT. 23:31 MARK 15:15-20
LUKE 23:25 JOHN 19:1-16

Pilate's House — FRIDAY MORNING

PILATE TOOK JESUS AND SCOURGED HIM.

WITH HIS STRIPES WE ARE HEALED.
ISAIAH 53:5

THE SOLDIERS BROUGHT JESUS INTO THE PALACE COURTYARD. THE WHOLE TROOP OF SOLDIERS GATHERED AROUND HIM.

THE SOLDIERS TOOK OFF HIS CLOTHES AND PUT A SCARLET CLOAK ON HIM. THEY BRAIDED A CROWN OF THORNS AND PLACED IT ON HIS HEAD. THEY PUT A STICK INTO HIS RIGHT HAND.

THEY WENT TO JESUS, KNEELED BEFORE HIM, AND MOCKED HIM AS THEY GREETED HIM—

HAIL, KING OF THE JEWS!

THEY TOOK THE STICK AND STRUCK HIM ON THE HEAD WITH IT.

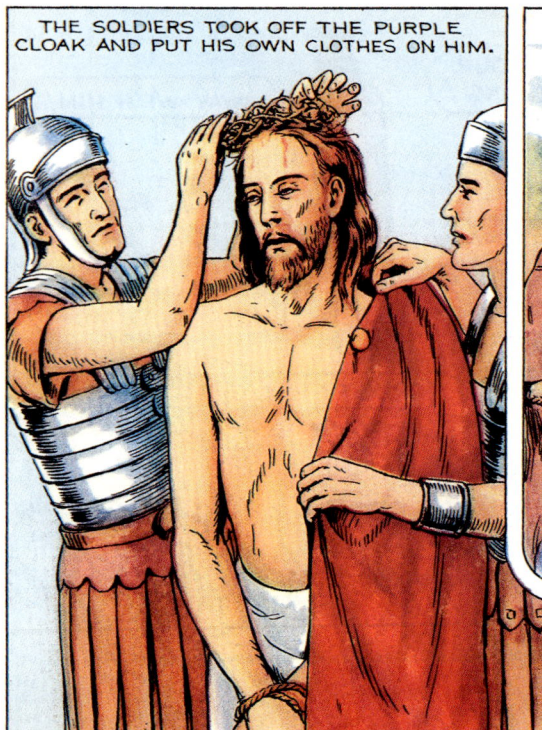

The court trial is over. Jesus is condemned to die on a cross for the sins of all mankind.

NOW, WHEN THE SOLDIERS HAD CRUCIFIED JESUS, THEY TOOK HIS CLOTHES AND DIVIDED THEM INTO FOUR PARTS, ONE FOR EACH SOLDIER, DRAWING LOTS TO SEE WHAT EACH ONE SHOULD TAKE.

THE TUNIC HAD NO SEAM. IT WAS WOVEN IN ONE PIECE FROM TOP TO BOTTOM.

LET US NOT TEAR IT, BUT DRAW LOTS TO SEE WHO GETS IT.

SO THE WORDS OF THE BIBLE CAME TRUE —

They divided My clothes among them and for My garment they drew lots.

Ps. 22:18

THEN THEY SAT DOWN AND KEPT WATCH OVER HIM.

PILATE ALSO HAD WRITTEN THE REASON WHY JESUS WAS PUNISHED. THEY HAD PLACED IT ABOVE HIS HEAD ON THE CROSS. HE HAD WRITTEN: "THIS IS JESUS OF NAZARETH, THE KING OF THE JEWS."

IT WAS WRITTEN IN

ARAMAIC... ישוע הנצרי מלכא דיהודא

LATIN.... HIC EST IESUS REX IUDAEORUM

AND GREEK... Ο ΒΑΣΙΛΕΥΣ ΤΩΝ ΙΟΥΔΑΙΩΝ

Jesus hangs on the cross for six hours. During that time He speaks seven times. Finally He dies.

AFTER HE SAID THAT, HE BOWED HIS HEAD AND GAVE UP HIS SPIRIT

JUST THEN THE CURTAIN IN THE TEMPLE WAS TORN IN TWO, FROM TOP TO BOTTOM,

THE EARTH SHOOK, THE ROCKS SPLIT, THE GRAVES OPENED, AND MANY BODIES OF HOLY PEOPLE WHO HAD FALLEN ASLEEP CAME BACK TO LIFE. THEY CAME OUT OF THE GRAVES AFTER HE HAD RISEN, CAME INTO THE HOLY CITY, AND SHOWED THEMSELVES TO MANY PEOPLE.

THE CENTURION SAW HOW JESUS GAVE UP HIS SPIRIT, AND HE PRAISED GOD—

THIS MAN CERTAINLY WAS RIGHTEOUS!

HE CERTAINLY WAS THE SON OF GOD!

ALL THE FRIENDS OF JESUS WERE STANDING THERE, AND MANY WOMEN WHO HAD FOLLOWED AND SERVED JESUS WHEN HE WAS IN GALILEE. THEY HAD COME UP TO JERUSALEM WITH HIM. NOW THEY WATCHED HIM FROM A DISTANCE.

HE AND HIS MEN SAW THE EARTHQUAKE AND THE OTHER THINGS THAT HAPPENED AND WERE VERY MUCH AFRAID.

MARY OF MAGDALA

Friends of Jesus now come to bury Him. Jesus' grave is near to where He died on the cross.

WHEN ALL THE PEOPLE SAW WHAT HAPPENED, THEY BEAT THEIR BREASTS AND TURNED BACK.

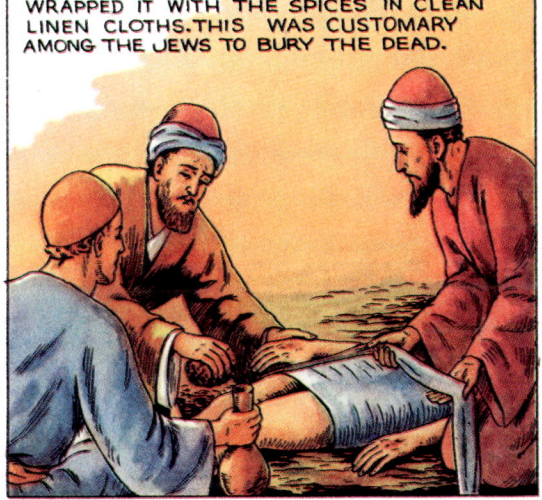

The sun is about to rise on the third day. The women are on the way to the tomb of Jesus. They would be surprised by what happened.

Jesus is alive. Many people will see Jesus alive. This brings joy and hope into the lives of many people.

BIBLE STORIES in PICTURES
by W. F. BECK
ILLUSTRATED BY RUTH W. ROGERS

JESUS LIVES!

A Garden near Jerusalem • EASTER MORNING, APRIL 9, 30 A.D.

MATT. 28:9-10; MARK 16:9-11; LUKE 24:9-12; JOHN 20:3-18.

MARY HAD TOLD PETER AND JOHN

"THEY HAVE TAKEN THE LORD OUT OF THE GRAVE, AND WE DO NOT KNOW WHERE THEY HAVE LAID HIM."

PETER AND THE OTHER DISCIPLE STARTED OUT ON THE WAY TO THE GRAVE. BOTH RAN TOGETHER.

BUT THE OTHER DISCIPLE RAN FASTER THAN PETER AND WAS THE FIRST TO COME TO THE GRAVE.

HE LOOKED IN AND SAW THE LINEN CLOTHS LYING THERE. BUT HE DID NOT GO IN.

Jesus now shows He is alive to two of His followers. They and we can now be sure that Jesus lives.

Jesus now shows all of His disciples that He is alive. We believe that Jesus lives even though we have not seen Him.

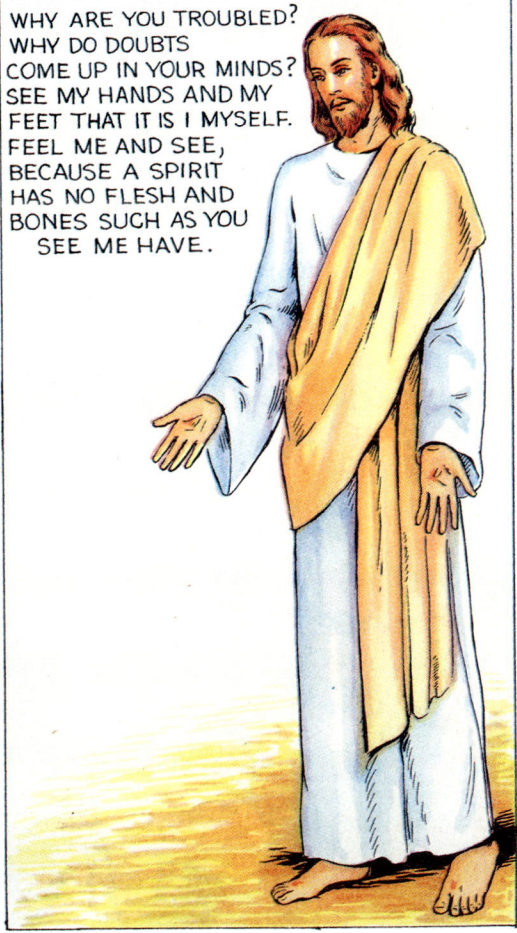

Jesus continues to meet with His disciples. From Jerusalem we now go to the Sea of Galilee. There we meet Jesus assuring Peter that he is His disciple.

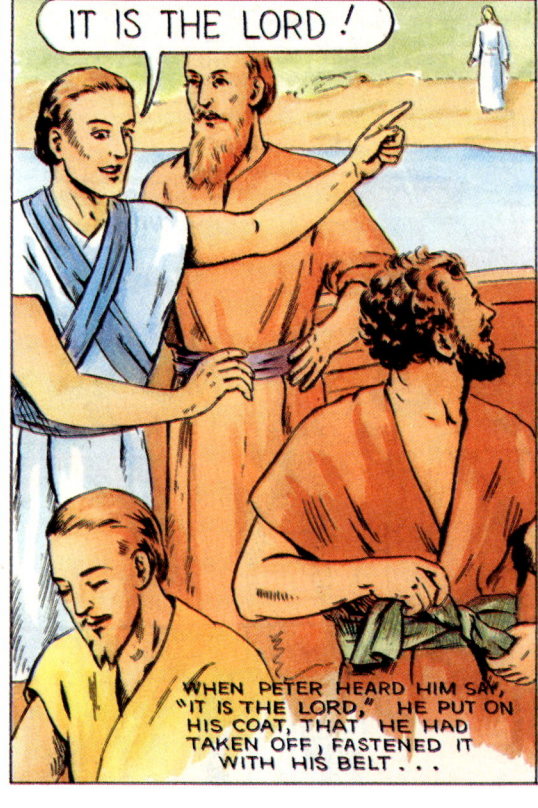

Jesus is ready to return to heaven. He now tells all His followers to tell the people of the world that He is the Son of God.

Jesus meets seven of His disciples while they are fishing. He performs the miracle of providing many fish. Once again Jesus shows He is the Son of God.

THEN THEY WENT BACK TO JERUSALEM WITH GREAT JOY.

JESUS ALSO DID MANY OTHER THINGS, ALSO MANY OTHER MIRACLES BEFORE HIS DISCIPLES, WHICH ARE NOT WRITTEN IN THIS BOOK. IF EVERY ONE OF THESE WERE WRITTEN, I THINK THE WORLD WOULD NOT HAVE ROOM FOR THE BOOKS THAT WOULD BE WRITTEN.

The Gospel as told by MATTHEW

The Gospel as told by MARK

The Gospel as told by LUKE

The Gospel as told by JOHN

BUT THESE ARE WRITTEN THAT YOU MAY BELIEVE JESUS IS CHRIST, THE SON OF GOD, AND BY BELIEVING MAY HAVE LIFE IN HIS NAME.

THE DISCIPLES WERE ALL TOGETHER IN ONE PLACE. SUDDENLY A SOUND AS OF A RUSHING MIGHTY WIND CAME FROM HEAVEN AND FILLED THE WHOLE HOUSE WHERE THEY WERE SITTING.

AND THEY SAW TONGUES AS OF FIRE, SEPARATING AND RESTING ON EACH OF THEM. THEY WERE ALL FILLED WITH THE HOLY SPIRIT...

THEY BEGAN TO SPEAK IN OTHER LANGUAGES AS THE SPIRIT GAVE THEM THE ABILITY TO SPEAK.

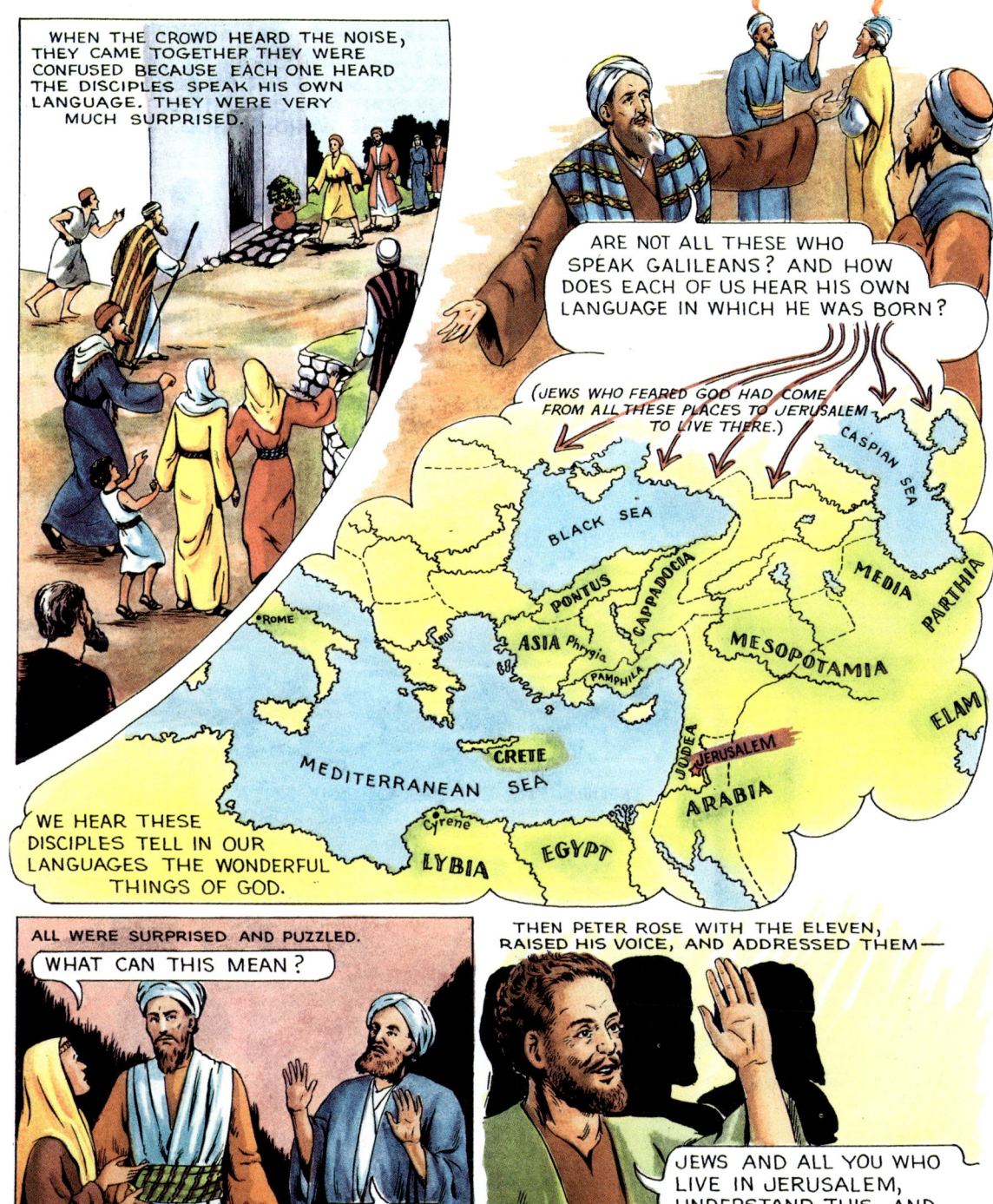

The disciples heal a man who could not walk. They continue to preach and teach about Jesus, the Savior of all people.

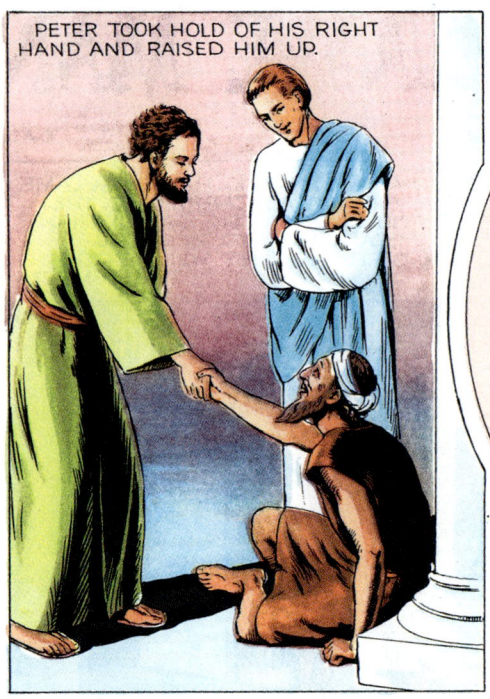

ON TRIAL
ACTS 4:1-31

BIBLE STORIES in PICTURES
by W. F. BECK
ILLUSTRATED BY RUTH W. ROGERS

Jerusalem 30 A.D.

WHILE PETER AND JOHN WERE SPEAKING, THE PRIESTS, THE CAPTAIN OF THE TEMPLE, AND THE SADDUCEES STEPPED UP TO THEM, MUCH ANNOYED BECAUSE THEY WERE TEACHING THE PEOPLE AND PREACHING THAT IN JESUS THERE IS A RESURRECTION OF THE DEAD.

THEY ARRESTED THEM.

AND SINCE IT WAS ALREADY EVENING, THEY PUT THEM INTO PRISON UNTIL THE NEXT DAY.

BUT MANY OF THOSE WHO HAD HEARD THE WORD BELIEVED, THE NUMBER OF THE MEN ALONE ROSE TO ABOUT FIVE THOUSAND.

BIBLE STORIES in PICTURES by W. F. BECK, ILLUSTRATED BY ESTHER STEINMANN

PHILIP BAPTIZES A TREASURER
ACTS 8:26-40

32 A.D.

There was a man from Ethiopia, a high official of Candace, queen of the Ethiopians. He was in charge of all her treasures.

He had come to Jerusalem...

To worship...

And was on his way home, sitting in his chariot.

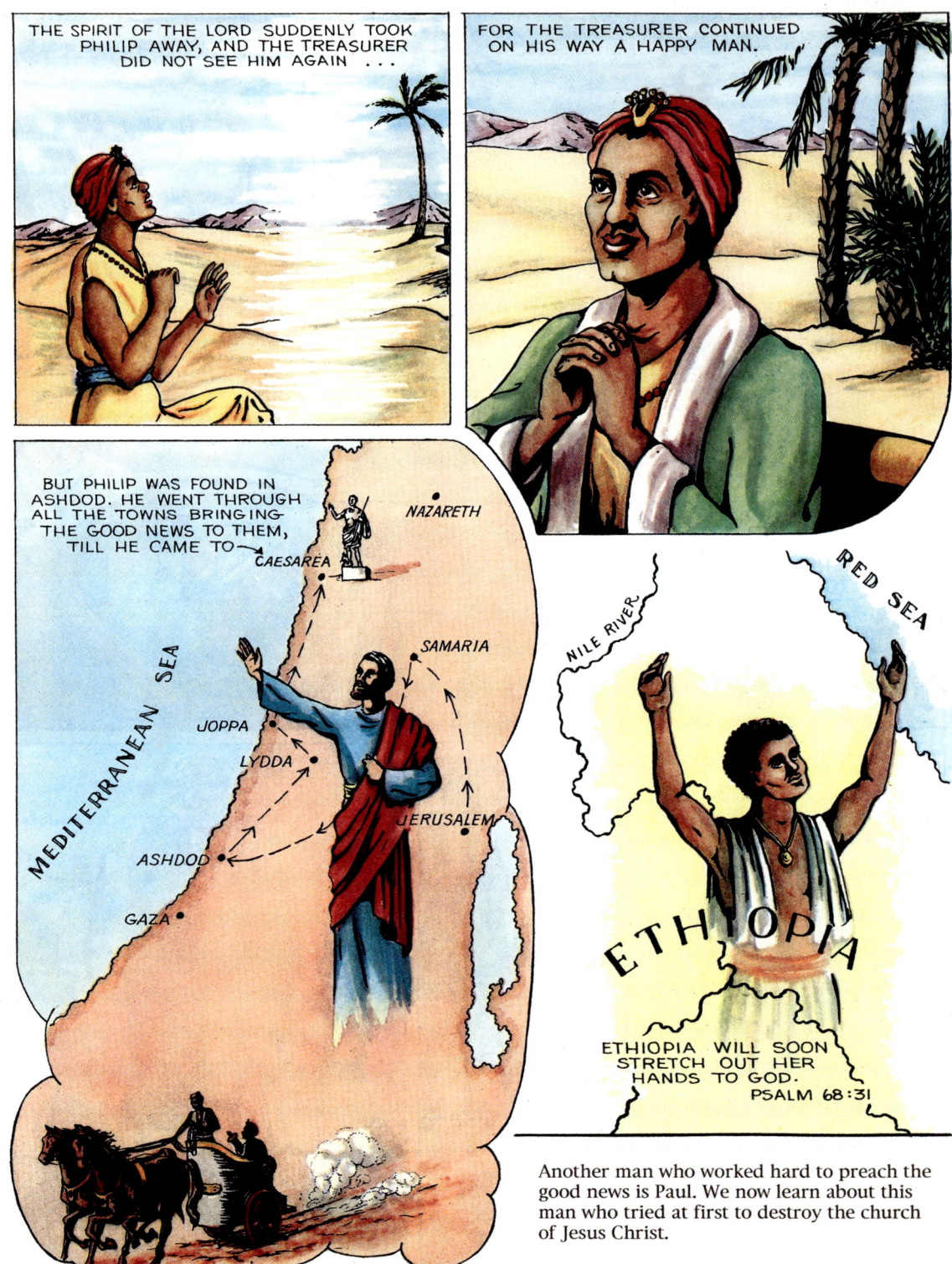

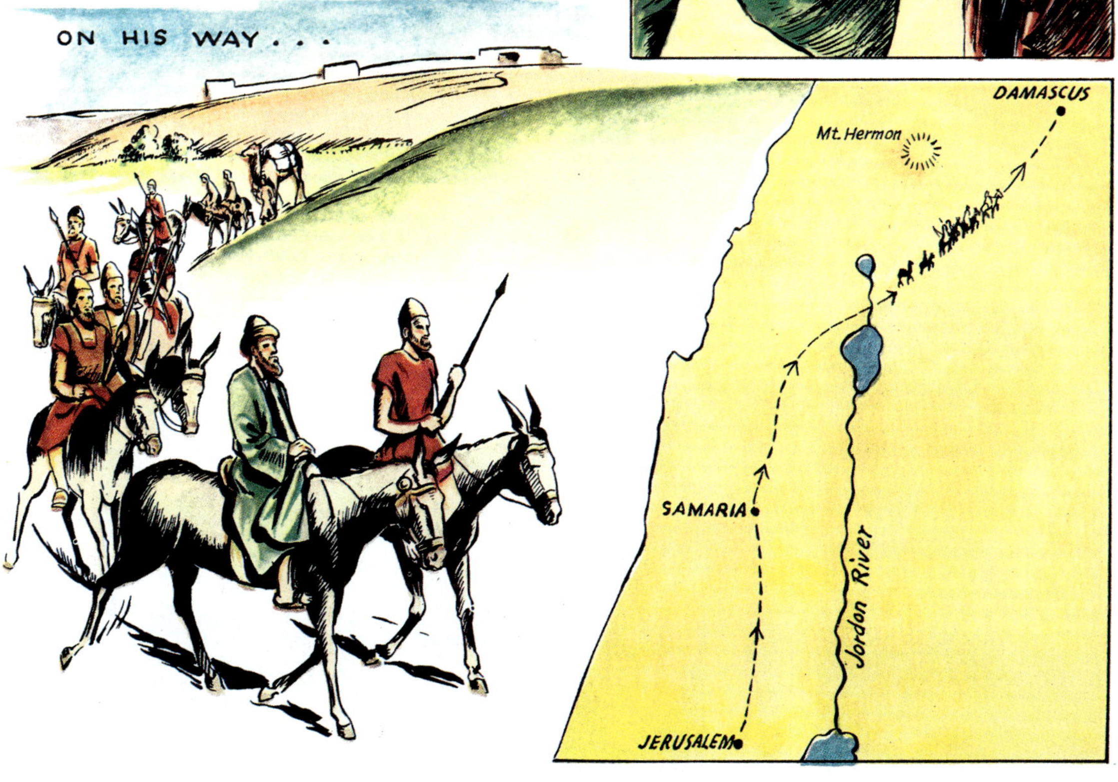

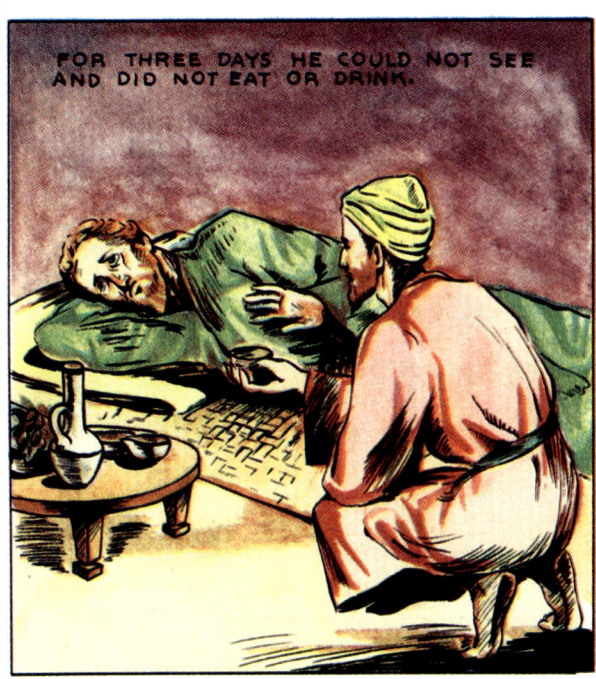

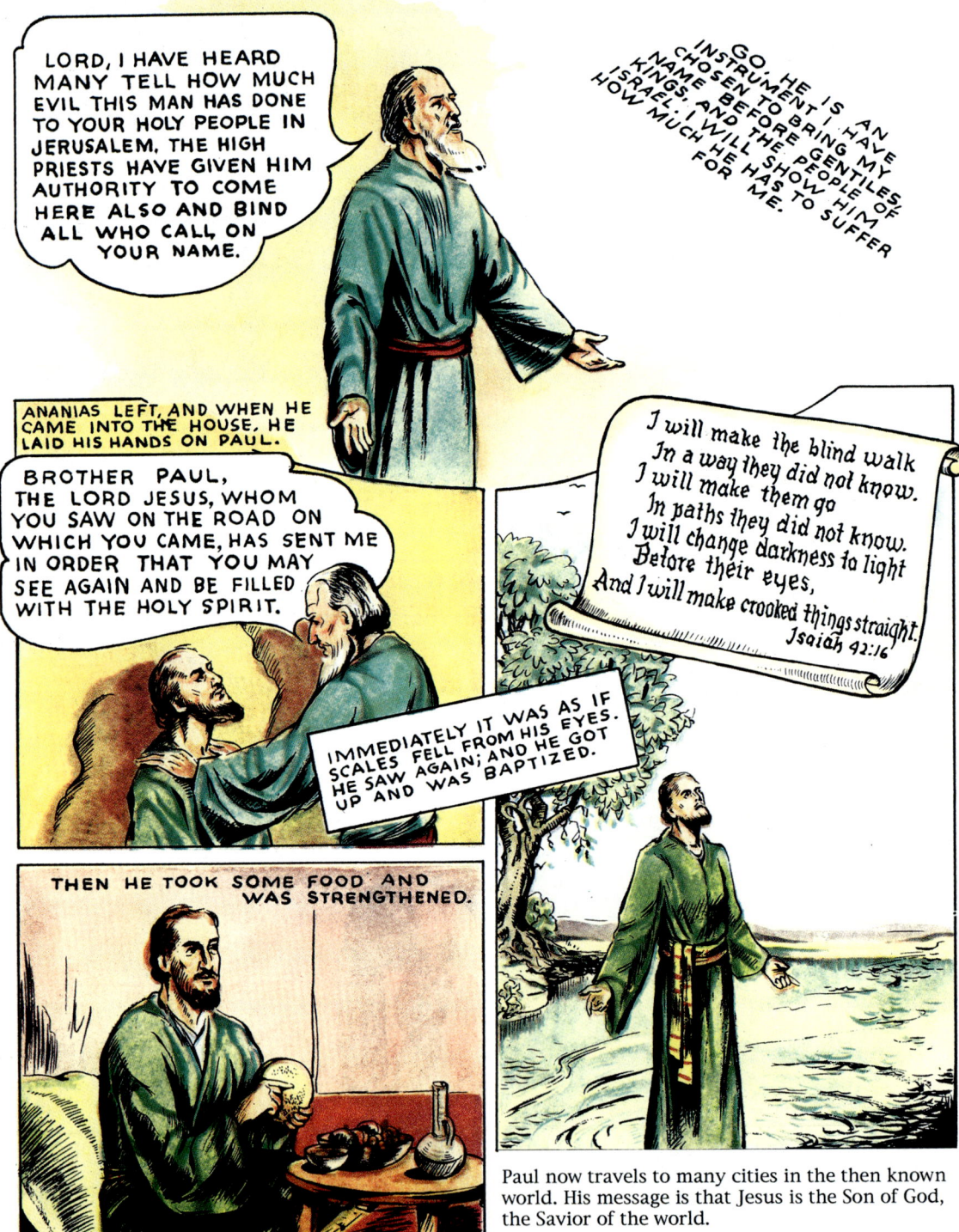

47 A.D.

BIBLE STORIES in PICTURES
by W. F. BECK
ILLUSTRATED BY RUTH W. ROGERS

ANTIOCH near PISIDIA
ACTS 13:13–52

PAUL, BARNABAS, AND MARK TOOK A SHIP FROM PAPHOS AND CAME TO PERGA IN PAMPHILIA.

THERE MARK LEFT THE OTHERS AND WENT BACK TO JERUSALEM.

BUT PAUL AND BARNABAS WENT ON FROM PERGA AND CAME TO ANTIOCH OF PISIDIA.

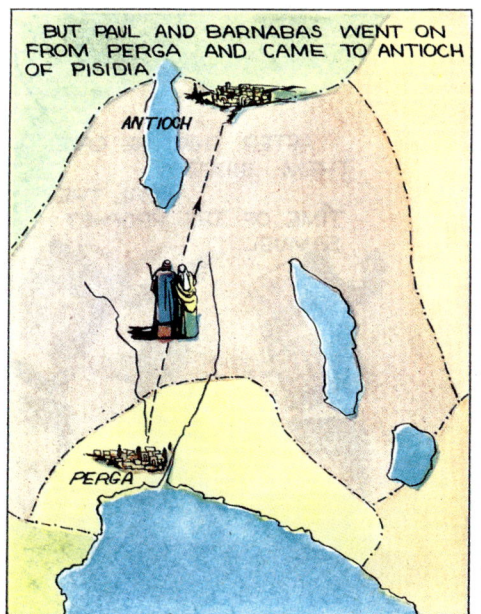

ON SATURDAY THEY WENT INTO THE SYNAGOG AND SAT DOWN.

Forgiveness of sins through faith in Jesus is the message Paul speaks to the Jews. But that is also the message God wants to be preached to those who are not Jews.

Paul now leaves to go toward Europe. The first city there is Philippi. The rulers of the city beat him and put him in prison. Learn what happens then.

Paul now travels to other cities. In Berea the people study God's Word to find out if Paul is telling the truth.

Thessalonica and Berea

ACTS 17:1-15; PHIL. 4:16; 2 THESS. 3:7-10

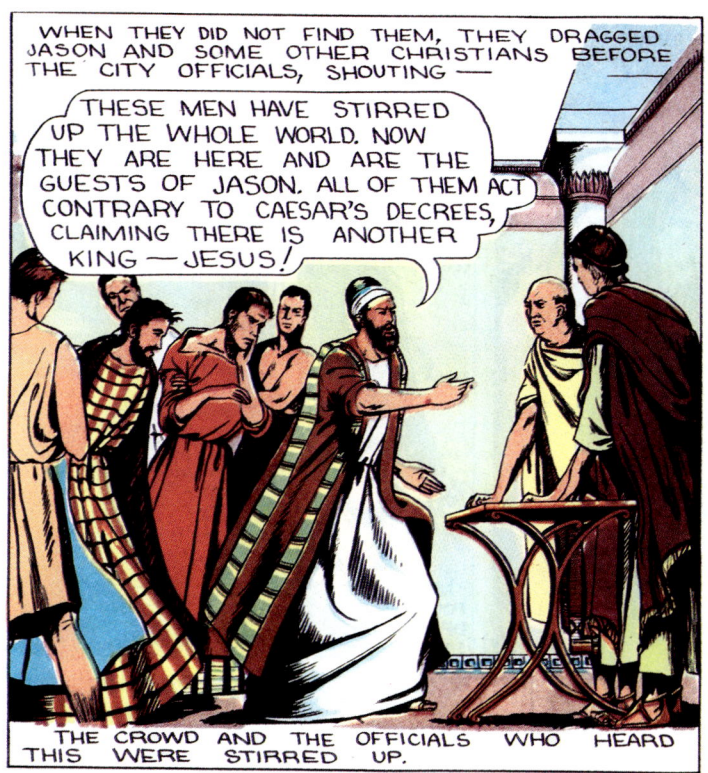

Paul performs many miracles. He revisits some of the churches he started. Then he goes to the city of Jerusalem.

Paul is the greatest missionary of the Christian church. He again revisits churches. He also brings to life a young man who died.

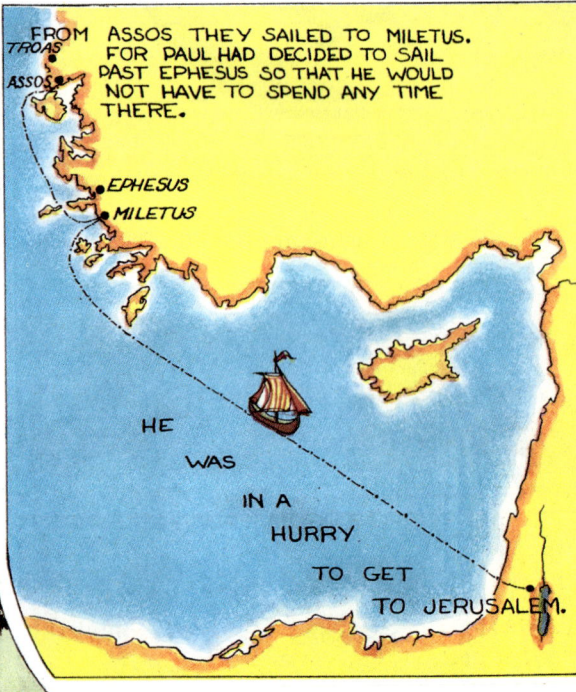

Paul shows his love to the believers. He continues to teach the good news about Jesus.

Paul was put into prison when he went to Jerusalem. He appealed to Caesar in Rome. After being a prisoner for several years in Rome, Paul was put to death.

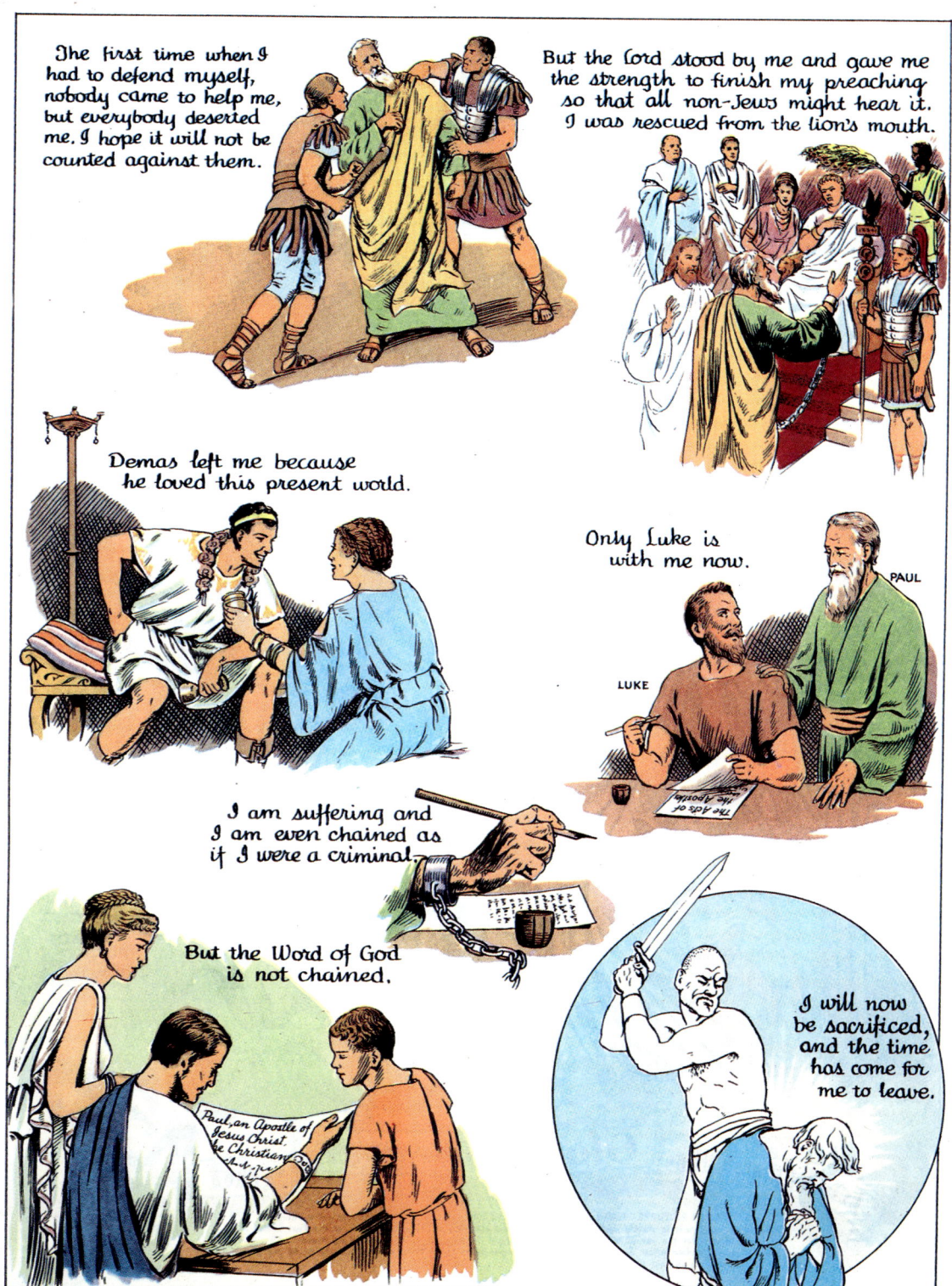